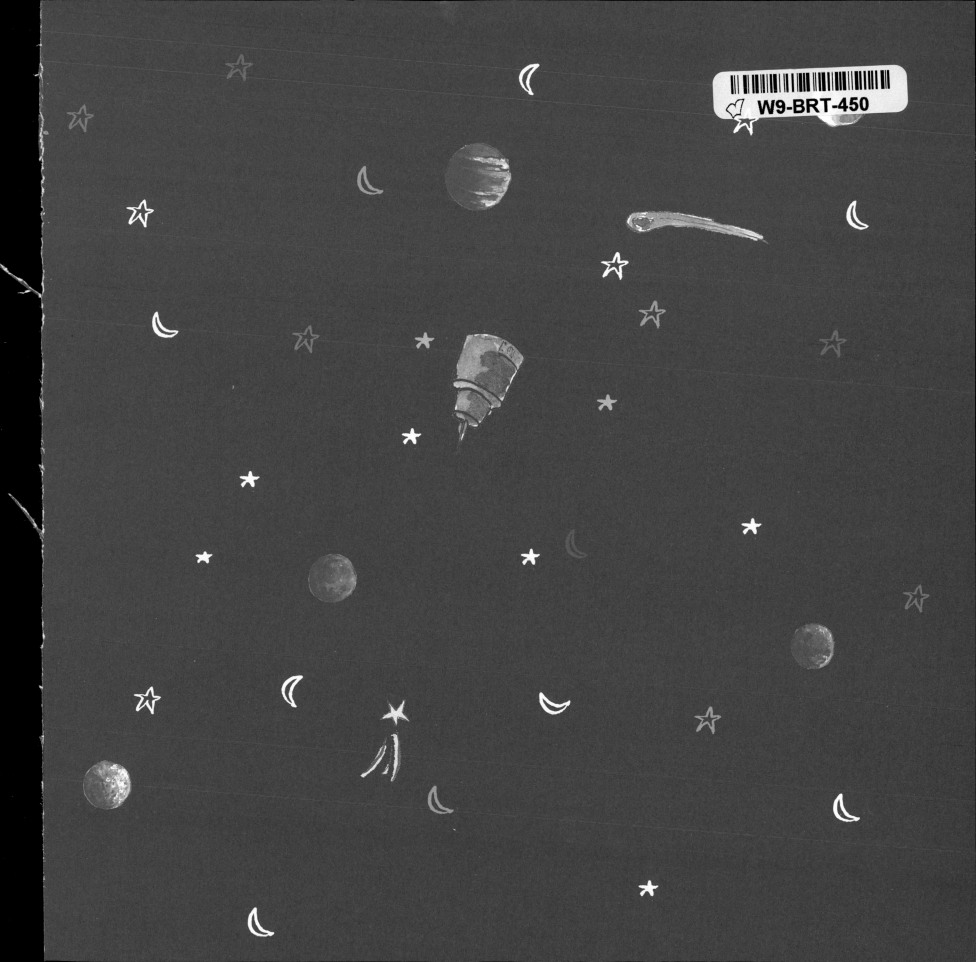

A CHILD'S INTRODUCTION TO

The Night Sky

A CHILD'S INTRODUCTION TO

The Night Sky

THE STORY OF THE STARS, PLANETS AND CONSTELLATIONS— AND HOW YOU CAN FIND THEM IN THE SKY

Michael Driscoll

Illustrated by
Meredith Hamilton

BLACK DOG
& LEVENTHAL
PUBLISHERS
NEW YORK

Photo Credits: Photos on pp. 9, 13, 17–18 (all), 39–40, 50–51 (all) courtesy of NASA/STSci; p. 13 courtesy of NASA/WMAP Science Team; p. 14 courtesy of Corbis/Dennis di Cicco; pp. 22, 26, 28, 29 (all), 34, 36–38, 42–44, 46 (bottom) courtesy of NASA/JPL/Caltech; pp. 30, 32 courtesy of Corbis/Roger Ressmeyer; p. 33 (all) courtesy of UCO/ Lick Observatory; p. 46 (top) courtesy of NOAO; p. 55 courtesy of Raw Talent Photo; pp. 60, 63 courtesy of NASA/NIX.

Black Dog & Leventhal Publishers
Hachette Book Group
1290 Avenue of the Americas
New York, NY 10104
www.blackdogandleventhal.com

Printed in China

Cover and interior design by Martin Lubin Graphic Design

First Edition: 2004

x w v u t s

Black Dog & Leventhal Publishers is an imprint of Hachette Books, a division of Hachette Book Group. The Black Dog & Leventhal Publishers name and logo are trademarks of Hachette Book Group, Inc. The Hachette Speakers Bureau provides a wide range of authors for speaking events. To find out more, go to www.HachetteSpeakersBureau.com or call (866) 376-6591.

ISBN: 978-1-57912-366-6

Library of Congress Cataloging-in-Publication Data

Driscoll, Michael.

A child's introduction to the night sky : the story of the stars, planets, and constellations—and how you can find them in the sky / Michael Driscoll; illustrated by Meredith Hamilton.

p. cm.

Includes index.

ISBN 1-57912-366-X

1. Astronomy—Juvenile literature. 2. Stars—Juvenile literature. 3. Constellations—

Juvenile literature. I. Hamilton, Meredith. II. Title.

QB46.D78 2004

520—dc22

20030280252

For Lucy

—M.D.

For my brothers, Eric and Randy, who patiently sat with me on summer nights, pointing out the constellations.

—M.H.

ACKNOWLEDGMENTS

The author and illustrator would like to thank the many who helped this book come about: J.P. Leventhal, for the opportunity; Laura Ross, for the guidance, perseverance and verve; Marty Lubin, for the wonderful design and contributions above and beyond the call; and Dara Lazar, for assistance in ways too numerous to count.

CONTENTS

Our Universe and Welcome to It

Have you ever looked up into the sky at night and wondered just what's up there? If you have, you're not alone—people have been wondering about the mysteries of the heavens for as long as there have been people.

What are all those shimmering specks of light, and why do they move across the sky throughout the night, and through the course of a year? What's the Moon doing up there, and why does it seem to change its shape each time we see it? How can you spot one of those cool-sounding "shooting stars" you've heard about—and what are they, anyway? (Here's a hint: They're not stars.)

Wonders of the Night Sky

The questions that the wide night sky poses are many. We've figured out the answers to lots of them through years—centuries, even!—of study and exploration. Brilliant scientists are working every day to answer many more. And often, the answer to one question leads us to wonder about another. But one thing's for sure: If there's an answer to every question we can come up with about the skies above us, it's going to be a long, long time before we uncover them all.

In this book we're going to learn a lot about all of the objects and forces that surround us, nearby and *waaayyyyyy* out there, and we'll meet the amazing thinkers who have unraveled their mysteries. We'll also hear some of the stories (sometimes called "myths") about monsters, gods and heroes that ancient people made up to explain the shapes they saw in the night. We'll read about the big ideas that scientists have come up with to explain all of the strange things we've witnessed overhead. And we'll learn about some of the mysteries that still remain. (There are plenty of those!)

Journey Into the Night Sky

There's lots to learn, but don't worry: we'll explore things one step at a time. Any tricky words we come across will be explained in the **Deep-Space Dictionary** all throughout the book. (And don't think of the words as hard, because once you learn them, they're fun to use—and you will sound like a real know-it-all when you share them with your friends and family!)

As we learn about the people who have studied the skies, they'll be featured in the **Astronomy All-Stars** sections throughout the book. Hey, there's our first new word to learn: **astronomy**. It comes from the word "astro-," which the ancient Greeks used to describe the heavens, and "-nomy," which means the study of something. So astronomy is "the study of the heavens." It's fitting that we'd use a Greek

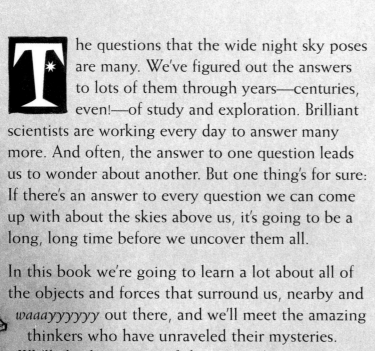

word, because the Greeks were some of the earliest people to examine the skies above. But more about them later.

For thousands of years, people peering up at night have spotted familiar shapes in the many points of light, as if the sky were a giant connect-the-dots puzzle. They saw people, animals and other figures, just like when you've looked up during the daytime and imagined a rabbit, a school bus or some other funny object in a fluffy cloud. You'll learn about some of those "myths": stories that early viewers thought of to explain what they saw when looking skyward. These legends helped people make sense of some of the mysterious things happening on Earth—like the seasons and the weather and earthquakes, and even wars.

But what fun is it to learn about those objects lighting up the night sky if you can't go out and actually find them? The **Sky Gazing** sections throughout the book should help with that. They offer instructions for pinpointing the many things you'll learn about.

The **Star Finder** will help with that, too. Tucked into the book's front cover is a special kind of map of the night sky that you can take outdoors with you. It even has glow-in-the-dark stars so that you can see better! Use it to pick out the many fun and interesting things you'll learn about. We'll find out more about using the Star Finder later, too.

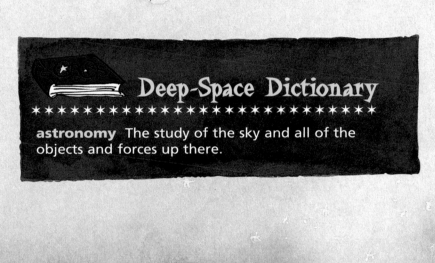

Deep-Space Dictionary

astronomy The study of the sky and all of the objects and forces up there.

THE UNIVERSE
The Big (Very, Very Big) Picture

Most of those bright dots you see when you look up into a clear night sky are stars—but some of them are planets. (We're going to learn the difference between the two, but when you see them at night, it's sometimes hard to tell which is which.) The stars and planets share the sky with other objects that we'll learn how to find, like comets, moons and meteors. There are many kinds of dusts and gasses up there in space, too. All of those things—the stars, the planets, the gasses—in fact, the Earth and everything on it, including dogs and cats and you and me—are part of the **universe**.

"Universe" is the word astronomers use to describe the biggest possible place they can imagine. It's where we live, where the Earth and the Sun reside, where all the stars call home and where everything we know of exists. It's so big our brains can hardly even imagine it. And no one knows *how* big it is. Most astronomers believe that the universe is at least billions and billions of miles across. They also think that it's around 15 billion years old.

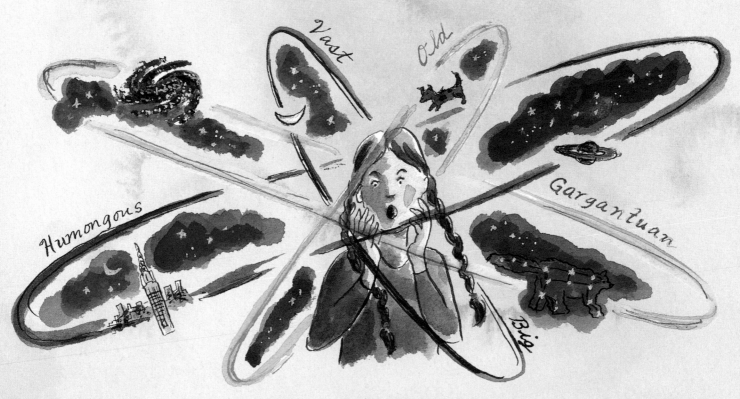

PONDERING HER PLACE IN THE UNIVERSE

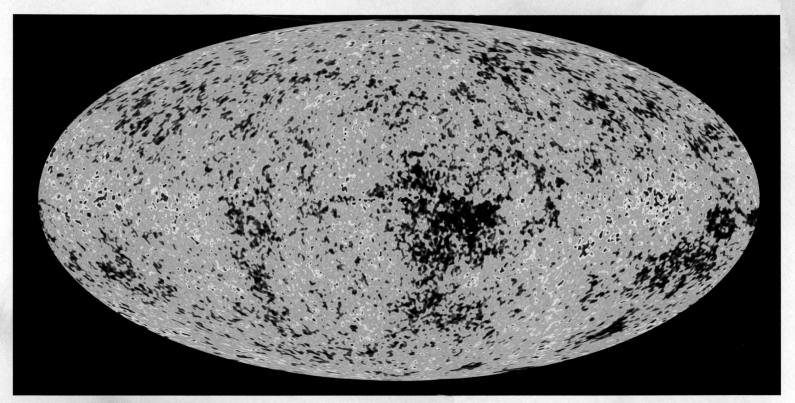

Scientists created this "baby picture" using light from when the universe was very young. Warmer areas show up as red and cooler areas as blue.

It has taken a long time for us to learn the things we know today about the universe. Early astronomers once thought the universe didn't extend much beyond the Earth. It was believed that the Sun and planets revolved around the Earth, and the stars were found just past the farthest planet from the Earth. It would be thousands of years before astronomers would figure out that the universe is actually much, much bigger.

But that's getting ahead of ourselves. Let's start our tour by taking a trip around the universe. The first thing we need to understand is . . . what's up there?

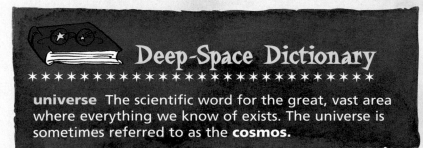

Deep-Space Dictionary

★ ★

universe The scientific word for the great, vast area where everything we know of exists. The universe is sometimes referred to as the **cosmos**.

Astronomy All-Stars

The Greeks get credit for their early astronomy, but they weren't the only ones studying the sky in ancient times. In fact, Chinese  astronomers made some pretty important discoveries as early as 1300 B.C.—hundreds of years before the height of Greek astronomy. The Chinese noticed that the stars moved across the sky in patterns that reappeared each year, and that the position of the Sun in the sky seemed to follow the same schedule. They used this information to create one of the earliest calendars we know about. It was a great example of making something very useful here on Earth out of information collected from watching the skies. It's hard to imagine life without calendars nowadays—how would we know when to throw ourselves a birthday party?

What's Up There?

Y ou probably know a little bit about the stars
and planets, and that's where we'll begin. But
there are other things up there, too. We'll also learn
about the great collections of stars called galaxies—
and especially <u>our</u> galaxy, the Milky Way. We'll study
the chunks of space rock known as asteroids; flying
objects called meteors, dazzling comets and lots more.
We'll even learn about some stuff that we can't see but
we think is there, like powerful black holes, mysterious neutron stars and that irresistible force known as
gravity. Along the way, we'll meet a lot of the really
smart people who observed objects in the sky,
thought hard about what they saw, came up with theories, tested them out and helped us understand a lot
about where we live and what surrounds us. First stop
. . . the stars!

What We Can See

THE STARS

Look up at the sky on a clear night and what do you see? **Stars**—what seems like thousands of them. In fact, you're seeing only those stars that are closest to the Earth. If our eyes had no limits, you wouldn't just be able to see thousands, you'd see *trillions* of them. How many is a trillion? A ten has one zero (10), a thousand has three (1,000). A trillion has *twelve* zeroes (1,000,000,000,000). That's a lot of stars!

But what exactly *is* a star, you ask? The easiest way to think of it might be as a giant ball of fire. Stars are great collections of gasses, like hydrogen and helium, that are slowly drawn together by the force of gravity. (We'll learn more about gravity later.) Stars contain other elements, too, like calcium and iron, but in smaller amounts. When it comes to exactly what's inside a star, and in what amounts, each one is a little different. When enough gas is collected in one place, the pressure causes it to begin to burn and glow. Then it begins to shine like the stars we see in the sky every night.

Once it has begun to burn, however, it can't collect any more gas. It burns off the gas it has inside for years—sometimes for just a "short" time, like a few million years, sometimes for a trillion years, or more. (Read on to find out why some stars burn longer than others.)

A Star Is Born . . . and (sniff) Dies

As you might suspect, stars (like our Sun, the closest star to Earth) are hot because they are constantly burning the gasses that are like fuel inside them. After many years, all that fuel is burned away, like when a car has used up all the gas in its tank and the engine sputters to a stop. Along the way, stars go through a number of stages.

Proto-Star   Brown Dwarf   Blue Giant   Red Dwarf

✳ Early in their development, stars are called **protostars**. At this point, they are not yet burning or giving off any light, but slowly growing heavier as dust and gasses come together in space. A real live star is about to be born.

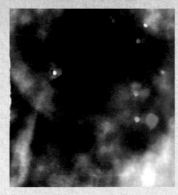

Protostars

✳ Once a star has gathered enough material and is packed tightly enough, it starts to shine and becomes a star as we know it. (A star that never reaches this point is called a **brown dwarf**. Instead of becoming shining balls of fire, these sad stars remain dark blobs of dust and gas, never quite managing to become brilliant flashes in the night.)

✳ As they get older, stars get bigger but burn less brightly, and are called **giant stars**. During their lifetime as stars, the hottest and brightest are called **blue giants**. They burn quickest, and stick around for only a few million years. A **red giant** has less energy, burns less brightly and can exist for billions of years because it goes through its fuel much more slowly than a blue giant. Our Sun is a fairly typical star in the middle of its life cycle, called a **yellow dwarf**.

Brown dwarf

Blue giants

Super Giant   *White Dwarf*   *Black Dwarf*   ✳ *Supernova*

★ The biggest stars, called **supergiants**, can grow to be 1,000 times the size of our Sun.

★ Before they burn out completely, some stars shrink to become **white dwarves**. When its fuel is burned out, a white dwarf becomes a **black dwarf**.

A white dwarf is formed

★ Bigger stars have a more spectacular finish, exploding into **supernovas** instead of shrinking into dwarves. These brilliant bursts usually burn for just a few weeks, and are rare finds that excite scientists whenever they spot one.

Gaseous remnants of a supernova

It looks like one star, but its really two...

Star Attractions

Just like a *bicycle* has two wheels, a **binary star** is made up of two stars that circle around—or **orbit**—each other. One is usually much brighter than the other, and because they are so far away, the two stars often appear as one when seen from Earth. For example, the star known as Algol, a part of the Perseus group of stars, is a binary star. **Multiple stars** are like binary stars, except they are made of three or more stars that revolve in orbits around one another.

Scholars of the Night Sky

People who study the stars in the sky (and all the other objects up there) are called **astronomers**. It's easy to get started as an astronomer. Just wait until the Sun goes down and point your chin up—that's

how the first star gazers got started thousands of years ago. These early astronomers used little more than their eyes and their minds, and were able to learn an incredible amount just from that.

The first sky watchers noticed that those tiny dots of light—the stars—seemed to move across the sky throughout the night, and to change positions as the seasons changed. They observed the movement of the Sun and Moon, too. Five thousand years ago, people in Europe built giant stone structures to track those movements. Stonehenge, an especially famous example of these structures, can still be visited today in England. On the other side of the world, pyramid-shaped structures built by the Mayan people in Central America are also thought to have been used to study the heavens.

The Chinese were scanning the skies, too. Around 350 B.C., a Chinese star watcher named Shih Shen recorded information about 800 stars in the first book of its type. Astronomers in Egypt, the Middle East and elsewhere were also studying the stars. It was, and still is, a worldwide fascination.

Over the next thousand years, the Greeks took the lead in the study of astronomy. Scholars with tricky names like Hipparchus (*hip-ARK-us*), Aristarchus (*air-is-TARK-us*) and Eratosthenes (*air-a-TOS-tha-*

Stories of the Stars

It's natural to make up stories to explain things you don't understand. People have been doing it for thousands of years. Some especially fantastic tales have been told to explain how the stars got into the heavens.

Native Americans in the Pacific Northwest region of the United States believed that at one time, the sky was entirely dark—too dark. As they tell the story, a youngster named One Who Walks All Over the Sky made a mask out of wood and set it on fire. Every day he travels across the sky, and the Sun that we see shining is actually his blazing mask. (One Who Walks All Over the Sky must have had a special face—one that couldn't burn—to match his special mask.) At night, he sleeps below the horizon—the imaginary line where the sky meets the surface of the Earth. As One Who Walks All Over the Sky snores, sparks fly out of his mask and light up the night sky as stars.

knees) used their observations to speculate about the size of the Earth, its distance from the Sun and Moon, and the distance between other objects in the sky.

In Europe, interest in the stars seemed to fade for a time after the age of the great Greek astronomers. But some still worked to answer the many great

Deep-Space Dictionary

✦✦✦✦✦✦✦✦✦✦✦✦✦✦✦✦✦✦✦✦✦✦✦✦✦✦✦✦

star A huge ball of burning gas in space, sometimes so large that it makes our own Sun look like a pinprick in comparison.

protostar The stage in a star's development when its dust and gasses are still coming together, before it begins to shine.

brown dwarf A cluster that never gathered enough dust and gas to become a shining star.

blue giant A very hot, very bright star in the middle of its life cycle.

red giant A star in the middle of its life cycle that is cooler and dimmer than a blue giant.

yellow dwarf A star of average temperature and size in the middle of its life cycle.

supergiant The biggest of the red giant stars.

white dwarf A star late in its life cycle that is still burning but is shrinking and less bright.

black dwarf A white dwarf star that has burned up all its fuel and become a cold lump of the element carbon.

supernova A star whose life ends in a fast, spectacular explosion rather than becoming a dwarf star.

orbit The path one object, like a planet, takes around another object, like a star. The Earth orbits around the Sun approximately about once every 365 days—that's how we measure one year.

binary star Two stars that orbit each other and often look from a distance like one star.

multiple star Three or more stars orbiting around one another.

astronomer Someone who studies stars and other objects in the sky.

telescope A special instrument, made with lenses and mirrors, that helps us see faraway objects such as stars and planets by making them look closer.

light-year The distance light travels in one year, or about 5.8 trillion miles (9.3 trillion km).

questions about the skies above. In Persia, around the year 1000 A.D., the Arabic astronomer al-Sufi became the first person to spot a galaxy beyond our own—the Andromeda (*an-DRAH-mi-dub*) galaxy.

Five hundred years later, astronomers in Europe wrestled with a question that seems easy to answer today—whether the Sun and planets revolved around the Earth, or whether the Earth and the other planets revolved around the Sun. Some of the smartest scientists around thought that the Sun was at the center of everything, but for thousands of years people had assumed that the Earth was. It took many years and lots of research about the movement of the Sun, Moon and planets to finally convince everyone. (Although there's probably *someone* out there who still thinks the Earth is the center of it all!)

A giant leap in the study of the stars came around the year 1600, when Galileo Galilei perfected the **telescope**—a device that uses lenses, and sometimes mirrors, to make faraway objects appear closer—and used it to examine the heavens. Many of the telescopes astronomers use today are based on the same basic model and techniques used by Galileo. With them, astronomers have discovered ever more objects up in space, and learned more and more about the things they've found.

Light-Years: A Bright Idea

A baby's height is first measured in inches (or centimeters). As she grows up, and the distance from the tip of her toes to the top of her head gets longer, we switch to measuring her in feet so as not to get confused by all those inches. One day that baby (now a young girl) starts riding a bike to her friend's house, and pretty soon we're measuring distances in miles rather than feet.

But what about when even miles seem too small? As we've learned already, space is big, and even the closest things may be billions of miles (or kilometers) apart.

To avoid tacking all of those zeroes onto our numbers, we needed a MUCH bigger unit of measurement. That's what led astronomers to come up with the **light-year**. The first thing that's tricky about the light-year is its name. We all know a year is a unit of time, but a light-year measures *distance*—the distance that light travels in one year. (Get it?)

When you turn on a switch and a lamp brightens on the other side of the room, it looks as though both happen at the same instant. But in fact,

① On Earth, Hubert flips on his bedroom light.

the light turns on a tiny fraction of a second before you see it, because it takes time for the rays of light to get from the lamp to your eyes. In your living room, that amount of time is so short that you don't even notice it. But it can take quite a long time for light to travel across the vast distances of space.

② 4 years and 5 weeks later, on Alpha Centauri, someone or something sees the light.

To be precise, it takes one full year for light to go 5.8 trillion miles (9.3 trillion km). (That's about equal to 750 round-trip journeys from the Sun to Pluto.) Because it takes so long for light to travel, by the time it reaches us, the things we're seeing may have happened long ago. In other words, if a light were to flash in space one light year away from Earth (or 5.8 trillion miles), we wouldn't see its glimmer until a year later. Now that's far!

It's a tricky concept, but it's an important one to remember. When we're looking at stars, not only are we seeing something far away, we're seeing something—depending on just how far away—that may have happened a long, long time ago. If a star five light-years away were suddenly to go dark today, we wouldn't see it flicker off for another five years.

A Star to Call Our Own
THE SUN

Because it shines during the daytime, you might not have thought of the Sun as a star. But it *is* a star, and it's the one we're most familiar with. The Sun lights up the day, keeps us warm (even at night when we can't see it) and offers beautiful sunsets. It is huge, especially when compared to the size of Earth. The sun's **diameter** (or its width through the middle) is more than 100 times the diameter of our home planet.

And it's hot! The Sun is made up of gasses—mostly hydrogen, helium and oxygen—that burn at about 10,000 degrees Fahrenheit on its surface, and at nearly 30 million degrees at its core.

Still, despite its size and heat, the Sun is pretty average when compared to other stars. Some get much bigger. The star Antares (*an-TAR-ees*), which is part of the Scorpius group of stars we'll learn about later, is more than 1,000 times bigger than

our Sun. That means Antares is 100,000 times bigger than the Earth. To think about it another way, if the Earth were represented by a ball one inch wide, Antares would be about a mile-and-a-half wide.

Astronomers think the Sun has been shining for about 5 billion years and expect it to shine for about 5 billion more. Then it will grow into a red giant much bigger than its current size, before cooling off to become a white dwarf and, finally, a black dwarf.

Everybody knows you shouldn't stare at the Sun— and you wouldn't even *think* about looking at it through a telescope. But some fancy telescopes have special dark filters that allow you to look right at the Sun. When you do, you see more than just a ball of yellow. **Sunspots** are visible—cooler, darker areas that appear and disappear on the Sun's surface. (Some sunspots can actually be bigger than the Earth!) You also might see a **prominence**—a blast of gas shooting from a sunspot that can arc out for hundreds of thousands of miles. About every eleven years, the Sun becomes particularly active, and the number of prominences and sunspots increases. Sometimes as many as 100 sunspots can be seen at one time.

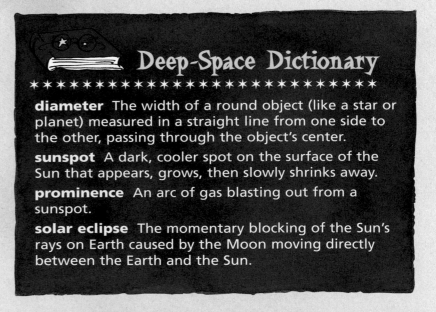

Deep-Space Dictionary

★★★★★★★★★★★★★★★★★★★★★★★★★★★★★

diameter The width of a round object (like a star or planet) measured in a straight line from one side to the other, passing through the object's center.

sunspot A dark, cooler spot on the surface of the Sun that appears, grows, then slowly shrinks away.

prominence An arc of gas blasting out from a sunspot.

solar eclipse The momentary blocking of the Sun's rays on Earth caused by the Moon moving directly between the Earth and the Sun.

Sky Gazing

Two or three times each year, the Earth, Moon and Sun get into alignment for an eclipse somewhere on the Earth. Because of the planet's rotation, however, the location on the Earth where the total eclipse is visible changes. Keep an eye out for when the next eclipse is due in your area.

There are several ways to get a great view of a solar eclipse. If you've got access to a fancy telescope, you can use special lenses to filter out the Sun's light. An easier way is to use extra-dark sunglasses, which sometimes can be bought around the time a big eclipse is expected, or at stores that sell astronomy equipment. Or, try poking a tiny pinhole in the side of a shoebox, then cutting a slightly larger viewing hole next to it. Once the Sun is lined up  to shine directly through the pinhole, you can see a tiny image of the Sun inside the box, complete with the Moon easing in front of it. It's like creating your own little movie inside the box, and is much safer to look at than the actual eclipse.

Who Turned Out the Lights?

A **solar eclipse** is one of the most breathtaking sights in the sky, and it happens frequently enough that you'll probably get to see one sometime.

When, on its journey around the Earth, the Moon gets into just the right alignment, it passes directly between the Sun and the Earth. The result is a blocking of the Sun's rays as the Moon slides in front of it, like someone slowly moving his or her

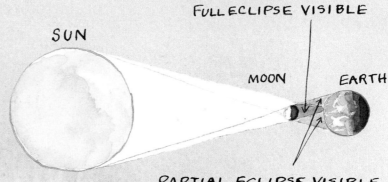

hand in front of a light bulb. It just so happens that, although the Moon is much smaller than the Sun, the two objects appear to be nearly the same size when viewed from the Earth because the Moon is so much closer. This fact is never more apparent than when the Moon eclipses the Sun.

A total eclipse, when the Moon completely blocks out the Sun, is an amazing sight. The moon slides completely in front of the sun, the sky gets dark in the middle of the day, and sometimes you can even see stars and planets. At this point (and at this point only!) it's okay to look at the Sun directly.

The Sun is never completely obscured for more than eight minutes during an eclipse, but it is quite an experience. People react in different ways. Some early viewers were frightened and thought that a dragon was eating the Sun, or that the world was coming to an end. Can you blame them? It is very strange to see night fall during the day!

CAVEMAN'S CONCEPT OF AN ECLIPSE

THE PLANETS

You probably already know that the Earth we live on is a planet, but do you know what planets are made of, and what makes them different from stars? Planets are large balls of rock, metal or gas that circle around a star. Only the very closest planets are visible from Earth. Unlike stars (like the Sun), planets (like Earth) don't give off their own light. Instead, they reflect the light of stars—although sometimes, when we look up at all the glowing objects in the sky, it's hard to tell the difference between a star and a planet.

The Earth and the rest of the planets orbiting the Sun are part of the **Solar System**—our own neighborhood within the Milky Way galaxy. Our closest neighbors in the Solar System are the Moon (which we'll learn more about a little later) and the eight planets that, along with the Earth, orbit the Sun: Mercury, Venus, Mars, Jupiter, Saturn, Uranus, Neptune and Pluto. Pluto is a little different from the other eight planets, but we'll learn a more about that later, too.

Neptune

Deep-Space Dictionary
****

planet A large ball of rock, metal or gas that circles around a star.
Solar System The system of planets and other objects orbiting around our Sun. ("Solar" means "relating to the Sun.")

At 36 million miles away, Mercury is closest to the Sun. If one million miles equaled one-tenth of an inch on this page, Mercury would be about three-and-a-half inches from the Sun. The Earth would be close to ten inches away. At 3.7 billion miles from the Sun, Pluto, the most distant planet in the Solar System, would be about 30 feet away—off the page, around the corner, maybe in your kitchen.

Jupit.

The planets have always held a special fascination for sky watchers. Because they revolve around the Sun, some planets seem to travel in strange ways across the sky, when viewed from Earth. Because they are closer to us than the stars, they're very bright. Many early viewers thought these spots of light had special powers, so they named the planets after their gods. Those are the names we still use today.

Keeping the Order in Order

One easy way to remember the order of the planets is to memorize this sentence: *My very educated mother just served us nine pizzas.* Each word begins with the same letter as a planet in the Solar System, in order from closest to the Sun:

Mercury,
Venus,
Earth,
Mars,
Jupiter,
Saturn,
Uranus,
Neptune,
Pluto

I Luv Mom

Saturn

Uranus

Venus SUN Mercury Earth

Mars

Astronomy All-Stars

The early Greeks (starting around 500 B.C.) were especially famous for studying the heavens. As the Earth rotated, they saw the Sun, the Earth's Moon and the planets moving across the sky. This led them to think that everything revolved in circles around the Earth. (Of course, this would later turn out to be wrong—but that's how science works: People learn new things all the time, and we are constantly updating what we believe is true.)

The Greek scientist **Ptolemy** (*TAHL-uh-mee*), who lived in the second century A.D., relied on the work of other Greek astronomers who had come before him when writing his books. Because of what he wrote, the idea of a universe with the Earth at the center and the planets and Sun revolving around it is sometimes called a Ptolemaic universe.

After the age of the Greek astronomers passed, scholars in the Middle East collected the information that was passed on to them, and updated it with their own findings. But the "next big thing" in astronomy didn't happen until around the year 1500, when a Polish astronomer named **Nicolaus Copernicus** (*ko-PURR-nick-us*) put forth the idea that Earth and other planets were in orbit around the Sun. This, he said, would explain why some planets seemed to move in strange ways as they crossed the Earth's sky, rather than in obvious circles, like the Moon.

At the time, religious and scientific beliefs were based on the idea that the Earth was the center of the universe, so many people didn't much care for Copernicus and his wacky new ideas. (I guess people like to think that they're at the center of everything.) It wasn't until many years later, after his death, that Copernicus' idea of the planets revolving around the Sun was proven to be right.

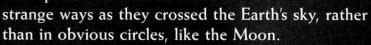

Pluto

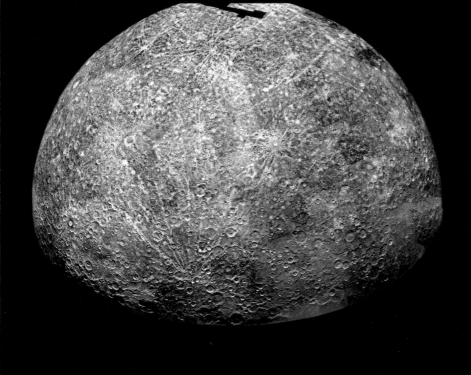

MERCURY
The Speed Demon

PLANETARY PARTICULARS

Diameter: 3,032 miles

Length of Day (or time it takes to make one full rotation): 720 hours (30 Earth days)

Length of Year (or time it takes to make one orbit around the Sun): 88 Earth days

Moons: None

Average Temperature: 332° F

he planet closest to the Sun, and the first stop on our tour through the Solar System, is Mercury.

Conditions on the planet Earth are perfect for our form of life, but we couldn't possibly live on Mercury. It is the second-smallest planet in the Solar System (bigger than only Pluto), and one of the least inviting. It has an **atmosphere** made mostly of nitrogen—none of the oxygen or carbon dioxide that is in the air surrounding the Earth. Standing on the surface of Mercury would be like stepping outside of the Space Shuttle in outer space—there would be nothing for us to breathe.

Much of what we know about Mercury we learned by sending the unmanned spaceships, known as **probes,** on drive-by visits. Although we've never landed on it, we've gotten close enough to see that Mercury's surface is similar to that of the Moon, which is dotted with wide plains and deep **craters,** holes made by objects that have crashed into its surface.

Some astronomers think that Mercury has an iron core that shrank when it cooled. This, they suggest, caused the surface to fold and wrinkle, which would explain how some of Mercury's cliffs and valleys came to be.

Mercury is hard to see in the night sky because it is so close to the Sun. (When Mercury is high up in the sky, the Sun usually is, too, and you can't very well hunt for stars and planets during the day.) Sometimes Mercury can be seen right after sundown or before dawn, when the Sun is just below the **horizon.** The best time to look for Mercury is when its orbit stretches the farthest from the Sun, but these times don't follow set dates on our calendar. Astronomy magazines and Web sites often list the best times to look for Mercury.

Rotate vs. Revolve

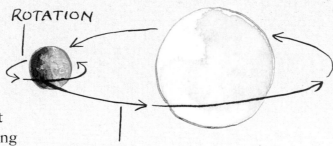

ROTATION

REVOLUTION

The planets in our Solar System **revolve** around the Sun, traveling along a path that brings them back to their starting point. While they revolve, they **rotate** in place, spinning in a circle like a merry-go-round. Way back when we were figuring out calendars, we decided that the length of time that it takes the Earth to revolve around the Sun would count as one year. It was decided, also, that the length of time it takes for the Earth to rotate on its **axis**, the imaginary line through its center, would be one day. So, our basic sense of time is directly determined by the rotation and revolution of our home planet.

Deep-Space Dictionary

atmosphere The air that surrounds the Earth or another planet.

probe A spacecraft launched from Earth and sent to collect information from distant places like other planets, asteroids or moons.

crater The hole left on a planet or moon by an object that crashed into its surface.

horizon The imaginary line off in the distance where the sky meets the surface of the Earth.

revolve (revolution) To travel around something else, as the Earth and other planets travel around the Sun.

rotate (rotation) To spin in place. The Earth spins or rotates at the same time that it is revolving.

axis An imaginary center line through a planet, around which it rotates. (The Earth's axis runs from the North Pole to the South Pole.)

Naming Mercury

Because it circled the Sun in only eighty-eight days, Mercury was considered a speed demon by early Roman sky-watchers. That's why they named the planet after the god Mercury, a figure in their mythology whom they believed had wings attached to his feet and to a helmet on his head. His super speed allowed him to carry messages back and forth quickly between the gods.

VENUS
Earth's Sister

PLANETARY PARTICULARS

Diameter: 7,521 miles
Length of Day: 243 Earth days
Length of Year: 225 Earth days
Moons: None
Average Temperature: 850° F

 enus is closer to the Earth than Mercury is, but don't get any ideas about it being a comfier place to live. Believe it or not, Venus is even hotter than Mercury!

People once thought of Venus, the second planet, as Earth's sister, because it is close by and nearly the same size as the Earth. But the two planets have little else in common.

The atmosphere of Venus is thick with clouds that make it impossible to see the planet's surface. They also trap in heat, like a sunny room with the windows closed and no fans or air-conditioning. This is what makes the planet so hot—even hotter than Mercury, despite the fact that Venus is about twice as far as

Mercury from the Sun. On its surface, Venus has giant volcanoes and vast plains that were made when lava spread and then cooled.

Venus rotates so slowly that its days are actually longer than its years. That means it takes longer for the planet to spin once on its own axis than it does for it to go all the way around the Sun. And Venus has an especially strange rotation—rather than rotating in the same direction as most other planets (counterclockwise), it rotates clockwise.

Astronomers think a powerful collision with a chunk of rock or metal that was floating through space, perhaps millions of years ago, may have set the planet spinning backward.

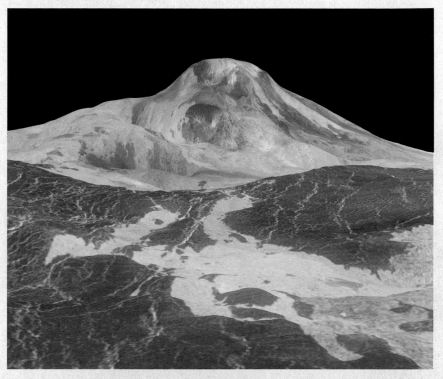

Lava flows from the Venusian volcano Maat Mons, named for an Egyptian goddess of truth.

Naming Venus

Early astronomers thought Venus' brilliant shine was especially beautiful, so they named the planet after their goddess of love. Almost every feature we've discovered on the planet's surface is named after a woman. It has a volcano named after the great Greek poet Sappho, and we call one region Phoebe, after another Greek goddess.

Looking past the moon, you can see Venus shining in the distance.

BOTTICELLI'S BIRTH OF VENUS
ITALY

VENUS OF MILO
GREECE

VENUS THE PLANET
OUR SOLAR SYSTEM

EARTH
No Place Like Home

PLANETARY PARTICULARS

Diameter: 7,926 miles

Length of Day: 24 hours

Length of Year: 365 days

Moons: 1

Average Temperature: 59° F

You probably don't think of the Earth when you think about space and the Solar System. But the Earth is a planet like any other—it's just the one we know the most about because we live here.

Two-thirds of the Earth is covered in water, and the rest of its surface varies from flat, dry deserts to towering mountain peaks. Earth has it all—we should consider ourselves lucky to live here!

More than 1.75 million forms of life have been identified on Earth, with more added every year. (Some scientists think there could be 100 million different forms altogether—that's a lot of bugs, bushes, bats and beetles!) And the Earth's atmosphere does more than just provide the oxygen humans breathe and the carbon dioxide that plants need. It also helps filter out the Sun's dangerous

rays, while allowing light to pass through and keep us warm, and brighten the sky so we can see.

So far, the Earth is the only planet that we are certain contains life. Most scientists think that's because it has plenty of water and doesn't get too hot or too cold. No other planet in our Solar

System shares these features, but maybe elsewhere, in some other galaxy, there is a planet where the conditions are right for life to exist. Considering how big we know the universe to be, it seems hard to imagine that there *isn't* life someplace out there.

It may come as a surprise, but the Earth is not perfectly round. The distance around the Earth from the North Pole to the South Pole and back is slightly less than the distance around the Earth at the **equator** (an imaginary line that circles the Earth precisely halfway between the North and South Poles). This means that the Earth is a little wider than it is tall—sort of like a ball of clay someone squished just a little too hard on top.

Astronomy All-Stars

When Copernicus figured out that the planets revolve around the Sun, it solved one of the great puzzles of astronomy. But later astronomers complained that the planets didn't seem to move in the perfect circles he described.

Tycho Brahe (*TY-ko BRA-hey*) was a sixteenth-century Danish astronomer who, like many at the time, still thought that the Sun revolved around the Earth. But his assistant, Johannes Kepler, used Brahe's research to reveal that the planets orbited the Sun in an ellipse. An ellipse describes something that is shaped like an oval rather than perfectly round. This discovery did a lot to convince people that Copernicus had been right all along.

Deep-Space Dictionary

★★★★★★★★★★★★★★★★★★★★★★★★★

equator An imaginary line that circles the Earth halfway between the poles.

THE MOON
Earth's Sidekick

LUNAR LISTINGS

Diameter: 2,160 miles

Rotates Around the Earth: Every 29½ Earth Days

Temperature: Ranges from -230° F to 220° F

You've already spotted the Moon lots of times, haven't you? The Earth's Moon is the easiest thing to find in the night sky, and one of the most interesting sights to explore. But what is it? Just as the Earth and the rest of the planets in the Solar System orbit around the Sun, a **moon** is an object that orbits around a planet.

We call the moon that orbits the Earth "the Moon," but it's not the only one that exists. In fact, most of the other planets in the Solar System have at least one moon orbiting them. We just call ours "the" Moon because it was the first one we noticed (and it's still our favorite).

The face of the Moon is covered with craters left by chunks of rock floating through space that crashed into its surface. You can see some of these craters when you peer up at the moon, especially when its whole face is shining. If you look closely (and use your imagination a little), you might be able to pick out what looks like a face—the famous "Man in the Moon."

How the Moon came to orbit the Earth is the source of much debate. Some think it was formed at the same time as the Earth. Others think it is a great chunk of rock that got caught in the pull of the Earth when it passed by the planet. Still others think it's the leftover material from a planet that once crashed into the Earth. We might never solve that one, but we know lots of other things about it.

The Moon is more than just a pretty circle in the night. Even though it's about 230,000 miles (384,000 km) away, it affects life here on Earth. Like all objects, the Moon has its own gravity—the natural force within every object that makes it pull on the objects around it. (We'll learn more about gravity later.) Water in the Earth's oceans is pulled toward the Moon, creating the tides at the beach. And the Moon's pull slows the Earth's rotation.

4 Days

First Quarter

10 Days

Full

18 Days

Last Quarter

26 Days

New

THE PHASES OF THE MOON

Scientists think that the Earth once spun all the way around in only eight hours, instead of twenty-four, before it was slowed by the Moon's gravity. Such a fast rotation made the winds blow much harder and the oceans' currents much stronger. If it weren't for the Moon, the Earth would be a much harsher place.

Lunar Eclipses

Instead of the Moon lining up between the Earth and the Sun, sometimes the Earth lines up in a perfectly straight line between the Moon and the Sun. On nights when this happens, we can watch as the Earth's shadow moves across the Moon. This is a lunar eclipse and, although it's not as dramatic as the solar eclipse you learned about earlier, it is still a fascinating and unusual sight.

Lunar eclipses require no special tools to see. As long as you know when one is supposed to occur, you can watch the Earth's shadow moving across the Moon simply by going outside and looking up at it.

Lunar Phases

Sometimes the Moon looks like a full, round circle, and other times you'll notice just a crescent-shaped sliver. This is based on the location of the Moon in relation to the Sun, and is referred to as the Phases of the Moon.

When the Moon is between the Earth and the Sun, the Sun shines on the Moon's back side, the side we can't see. This makes it appear totally black from Earth—we can't see it at all!—and we call this the New Moon. When the Moon is halfway on either side of the Earth, we see part of the dark side and part of the lit side. (As it's getting fuller, or waxing, it is called the First Quarter. As it's getting slimmer or waning, it is called the Third Quarter.) When the Earth is between the Moon and the Sun, we see the full, shining side of the Moon that is facing the the Sun—a Full Moon.

PARTIAL LUNAR ECLIPSE

FULL LUNAR ECLIPSE

MOON   EARTH   SUN

"Come to me oh weary waters..."

MARS
The Red Planet

PLANETARY PARTICULARS

Diameter: 4,222 miles

Length of Day: 24.6 hours

Length of Year: 687 Earth days

Moons: 2

Average Temperature: -81° F

If you were in a rocket ship traveling away from the Sun, you would encounter the planet Mars after you passed by the Earth. Mars has a few things in common with the Earth and a number of pretty big differences.

Mars has not one but two moons, although both are much smaller than the Earth's. Its day is slightly longer than ours—and Mars has water frozen in a northern ice cap, much like the Earth's poles.

But Mars' thin atmosphere allows a lot of heat to escape into space. That, combined with its greater distance from the Sun, makes the planet much colder than the Earth. The thin atmosphere also means that there isn't nearly enough oxygen to breathe, and it allows in lots of dangerous rays from the Sun.

The surface of Mars is covered with a grainy dust similar to the rust that forms on iron. Winds sweep the dust all over the planet, which gives it its red color. That's why we call Mars the Red Planet.

Martian Highs and Lows

Mons Olympus, a volcano on Mars that long ago stopped erupting, is the tallest known volcano in the Solar System. It towers 15 miles (25 km) into the Martian sky, and is three times higher than the tallest mountain on Earth. Mars also has the deepest known canyon—the Vallis Marinaris is more than 4 miles (6.7 km) deep, which means it's 3 miles deeper than the mighty Grand Canyon.

For centuries people have wondered whether life on Mars exists. In fact, a few billion years ago, the conditions on the Red Planet might not have been all that different from here on Earth. There's evidence that water once flowed across the planet in rivers and shallow oceans. Scientists think that the elements that made up the water may have slowly flowed into the atmosphere and then out into space, leaving the dry, dusty planet we see today.

Today, interest in our neighboring planet is building. In early 2004, there were five different spacecraft from Earth exploring Mars at the same time. European astronomers launched the *Mars Express* probe in June 2003. A little more than six months later, its high-powered cameras sent back photographs of features on the surface that scientists said could only have been carved by flowing water. It joined two American probes that were already circling the planet, *Mars Global Surveyor* and *Mars Odyssey*.

Meanwhile, *Spirit* and *Opportunity*, two American vessels (called "rovers"), landed on Mars and began slowly inspecting the planet's surface. Perhaps they'll find evidence that life once existed there. And, as if all the mechanical visitors weren't enough, on January 14, 2004, President George Bush announced a plan to send humans to Mars some day. If you are interested in becoming an astronaut, who knows? You might just be the first person to step onto the Red Planet!

Martian soil is high in iron oxide, or rust, which gives it its reddish-orange color.

Naming Mars

Because of its red color, early Romans associated Mars with blood, so they named the planet after their god of war. The Roman leaders kept what were known as the sacred spears of Mars in a special temple. When they went to war, the spears were shaken while one of the leaders shouted "Mars vigila!" ("Mars, wake up!")

The great Roman emperor Caesar Augustus considered Mars his personal guardian.

Sky Gazing

Like Venus and Mercury, Mars is best viewed just after sunset or before dawn. Every twenty-six months it makes a particularly close pass to Earth. That's the best time to look for it, and you can find those dates by checking an astronomy website or magazine.

JUPITER
King of the Planets

PLANETARY PARTICULARS

Diameter: 88,844 miles

Length of Day: 9.8 hours

Length of Year: 11.8 Earth years

Moons: 61

Average Temperature: -162° F

he planet Jupiter is much farther away from us than Venus is—about fifteen times farther, to be precise. But, like Venus, you can still find it in the sky using just your eyes. That's because it's so big— large enough to fit all the other planets inside and still have room to spare.

But in this case biggest doesn't mean best, at least if you're thinking about the best place to live. First of all, Jupiter doesn't even really have a surface to stand on. Deep in Jupiter's center is a core, but sur- rounding that are layers of gas. It's these layers that we see swirling around the planet. The temperature is not that cozy, either—even if you *could* find a sur- face to stand on, it would average around 100 or so degrees below zero. Brrrrrr!

Jupiter's most famous feature is probably its Great Red Spot, a giant storm sort of like a hurricane. (As if life on Jupiter doesn't sound miserable enough,

imagine being caught in that!) No one knows if the Great Red Spot will be around forever, but we know the storm has raged for at least 150 years. The first astronomers who used telescopes to take an up-close view of Jupiter saw the spot even back then. The Great Red Spot changes in size, and right now is almost 25,000 miles wide— or nearly four times as wide as the Earth.

One of Jupiter's most interesting features is its collection of moons—it has sixty-one! (And astronomers say there may be more we haven't found yet.) Galileo discovered the four biggest moons—Ganymede (*GAN-uh-meed*), Callisto, Europa and Io—and these are the ones that get the most attention from star gazers.

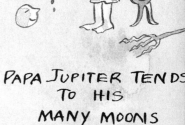

PAPA JUPITER TENDS
TO HIS
MANY MOONS

Jupiter is usually not too tough to find in the night sky, as it shines even brighter than the brightest star. (Aside from the Sun, of course.) It's easiest to see when it's closest, and in 2004, that's the first week in March. In 2005, it's closest during the first week in April; in 2006, during the first week in May; and in 2007, during the first week in June.

With a diameter of 3,270 miles, Ganymede is Jupiter's biggest moon. Like the Earth's Moon, it is rocky, cold and covered in craters with deep cracks and high cliffs.

Callisto has craters like our Moon, but not as deep. Scientists think these may be filled with ice. The newest craters have not yet filled in, and are brighter than the rest, giving the moon a splotchy look.

Although it has ice and rock like many other moons we've discovered, Europa is special because it appears to have water, too. Some astronomers think that the pull of the other moons' gravity may have something to do with why this liquid does not turn into ice.

Io is known for its many volcanoes, which continue to erupt. They spew out the chemical sulfur, rather than lava; enough to give it an entirely new surface about every hundred years.

The rest of Jupiter's moons are smaller, and have Greek names that are fun to try to remember and pronounce: Adrastea, Amalthea, Anake, Carme, Elara, Himalia, Leda, Lysithea, Metis, Pasiphae, Sinope and Thebe.

Naming Jupiter

As the largest planet in the Solar System, it's fitting that Jupiter is named after the supreme Roman god. But this is actually a coincidence—the Romans didn't know how big Jupiter was. They just gave it the name of their greatest god because the planet shone so brightly.

Jupiter

Io

Europa

Ganymede

Callisto

SATURN
The Ringed Planet

PLANETARY PARTICULARS

Diameter: 74,900 miles

Length of Day: 10.2 hours

Length of Year: 29 Earth years

Moons: 30

Average Temperature: -218° F

ext after Jupiter is a planet you're surely familiar with—the famous ringed Saturn. Those "rings" are actually bands of rock, dust and ice trapped in orbit around the planet.

Like Jupiter, Saturn is mostly made of gas—hydrogen with a little helium mixed in, to be precise—so you couldn't very well stand on its surface. Astronomers think that a spinning, rocky core is at its center.

But Saturn is best known for those rings of rock, dust and ice. Most of the objects are tiny (about the size you'd put in a glass of root beer), although a few may actually measure many miles in diameter.

Galileo first spied Saturn's rings in 1610 through one of his early telescopes. He thought they looked like tiny handles on the planet. Later scientists fig-

ured out that the bands were in fact rings, but mistakenly thought they were solid and thick. As it turns out, the spinning rings actually have a depth of only a few hundred yards (meters). Like many space questions, scientists aren't sure *why* exactly the rings exist. Some say they should have formed into a moon but never did. Others guess that they are pieces of a moon that was pulverized. Someday, we'll figure it out.

Deep-Space Dictionary
★★★★★★★★★★★★★★★★★★★★★★★★★★★★★★

dense Packed tightly together and often heavy, like a metal ball.

Sky Gazing

You'll need a telescope to see Saturn's rings, but the planet itself can be viewed with just your eyes. Every fourteen years the rings line up with Earth so that we're viewing them straight on, and can't see them at all, even with a telescope—sort of like looking at the edge of a flat piece of paper. If you happen to spot Saturn during one of these times, it will look like an ordinary planet. Try again the following year so you can see the rings!

Although it's not as well known as the red storm cloud on Jupiter, Saturn claims its own great spot. About every thirty years, a white spot appears in its atmosphere that astronomers think is a great storm much like the one on the next planet closest to the Sun. It sticks around for several months, then disappears for another few decades.

Saturn is the least **dense** of all the planets. (Something dense is packed tightly together, and usually heavy.) In fact, Saturn is so light that, if you were somehow able to dunk it into a giant bowl of water, it would float!

Naming Saturn

Saturn was named after one of the original Roman gods who fell from power. He was the father of Jupiter and a god of planting and harvests. The Greeks called him "Kronos" and considered him the god of time, so he is often depicted as a kind of timekeeper.

URANUS
Sideways Spinner

PLANETARY PARTICULARS

Diameter: 31,764 miles

Length of Day: 17.9 hours

Length of Year: 84 Earth years

Moons: 21

Average Temperature: -350° F

Peering up at the distant planet Uranus from the Earth (you'll have to use a telescope to find this one), the planet reflects a greenish-blue light. That's because of the mix of chemicals in its atmosphere.

Unlike many other planets, Uranus has a pretty steady temperature across the whole of the planet (and a cold one, at -350° F). Astronomers think there's little difference in temperature because of strong winds that blow around the planet in the same direction of its rotation.

There's one very unusual thing about Uranus: its axis is nearly in a straight line with its orbit, meaning it spins on its side! The Earth, and the other planets in the Solar System, all rotate pretty close to straight up and down, like a top does when you spin it on a table. (Each planet actually rotates a lit-

tle differently, and none in a perfectly straight line up and down, but you get the idea.)

Uranus is the only planet (that we know of, anyway) to rotate in this unusual sideways fashion. Its odd rotation means that, for one quarter of its orbit, its North Pole faces the Sun. Then its equator faces the Sun for another quarter of its orbit, followed by its South Pole. For the last quarter of its orbit, Uranus' equator faces the Sun again.

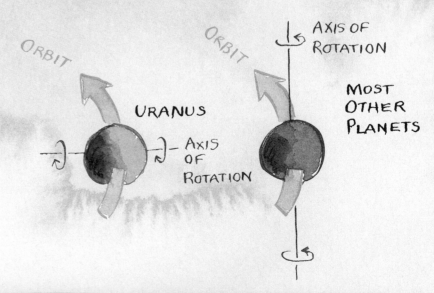

ORBIT ORBIT AXIS OF ROTATION

URANUS MOST OTHER PLANETS

AXIS OF ROTATION

Astronomers don't know why Uranus has such an unusual axis, but guess that a collision with something massive might have set the planet spinning sideways.

Astronomers believe that Uranus is made almost completely of gas, with just a tiny, rocky core—if it has a core at all. It is circled by more than a dozen moons, most of which were discovered when the *Voyager* 2 probe passed by in 1986.

Like its neighbor, Saturn, Uranus seems to have faint rings circling it, but astronomers are even less sure of what they are made of. As far as we can tell, the rings are made of boulders spinning in orbit around the planet. These boulders are part rock, part ice, part who-knows-what. Maybe someday we'll find out.

Planet X?

Astronomers have long thought that the orbit of Uranus was a bit strange. It doesn't seem to revolve around the Sun in quite the way they would expect, given the pull of the Sun's gravity. So they won-

dered if another planet was out there, its gravity pulling Uranus a little bit in its own direction. Neither Neptune nor Pluto (the next planets you'll learn about) fit the bill for this, so the question remains unsolved. Is there a mystery planet, the tenth in the Solar System, "Planet X"? If so, no one's found it yet.

Why not "Planet George"?

Naming Uranus

Uranus was discovered long after the age of Ancient Rome, but, in keeping with tradition, astronomers named it after a Roman god famous for science and discovery. The astronomer in England who first found Uranus wanted to name the planet after King George II, but astronomers from other countries didn't much care for that idea.

41

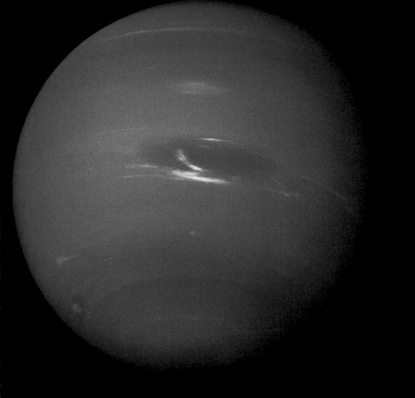

NEPTUNE
Big Blue

PLANETARY PARTICULARS

Diameter: 30,777 miles

Length of Day: 19.2 hours

Length of Year: 164 Earth years

Moons: 8

Average Temperature: -353° F

There are some pretty uninviting places to be in the Solar System (freezing on Mars or boiling on Venus, for instance), but if you're looking for a home besides Earth, Neptune might be the worst choice of all.

Not only is Neptune freezing, but its winds can thunder at up to 1,200 miles per hour. And it has huge storms like those on Jupiter. Add that, like Jupiter, Uranus and Saturn, Neptune is mostly made of gas, and you'll probably be glad you stayed on Earth.

Astronomers think Neptune may have a rocky core, but, as with Uranus, they're not sure. They do know that the planet has no real surface. Its atmosphere is loaded with methane, which absorbs red light, giving the planet the deep blue look it's famous for.

Three years after *Voyager* 2 whizzed past Uranus, it swung by Neptune and quickly spotted rings like those encircling Saturn and Uranus. But, unlike the boulders found orbiting Uranus, Neptune's rings seemed to be made up of dust-sized particles. *Voyager* 2 also got a close-up look at Neptune's eleven known moons. The moon Triton, which is nearly as big as the Earth's moon, is thought to be the coldest place in the Solar System: a chilly -393° F (-263° C).

Some astronomers think that Triton may have once been a planet. They say it passed a little too close to Neptune and became trapped by its gravity—but that is still a theory, not a fact that has been proven.

Another feature Neptune shares with its neighbors is a Great Spot. Jupiter has its red one, Uranus its white one, and Neptune boasts a Great Dark Spot. Astronomers believe it, too, is evidence of a huge storm.

A dark storm rages across Neptune's blue frontier.

Naming Neptune

Neptune was named after the god of oceans, lakes and rivers. (The story goes that he had a history of drying them out when he was in a bad mood!)

Trading Places

Pluto was considered the ninth planet from the Sun, but sometimes, its unusual orbit brings it closer to the Sun than Neptune. When this happens, for twenty years at a time, Neptune is actually the farthest from the Sun.

Though not as big as Jupiter or Saturn, Neptune (along with its neighbor, Uranus) is much bigger than the Earth—about four times as wide. History shows that it was discovered in 1846, but in fact, none other than Galileo spotted it in the year 1612. He mistook it for a star, however, and didn't pay the planet much attention. If he had, we might have known about our eighth planet almost 250 years sooner than we did!

Man, this is windy!

Sky Gazing

Because it's so far away, Neptune blends in pretty easily with any stars that happen to be nearby, making it tough to pick out. Binoculars or a telescope help. For the foreseeable future (until about 2015, anyway), the best time to look for it is in August.

PLANETARY PARTICULARS

Diameter: 1,429 miles

Length of Day: 6.4 Earth days

Length of Year: 248 Earth years

Moons: 1

Average Temperature: -356° F

Left: Pluto; right: Charon.

In 1930, Clyde Tombaugh (*TOM-baw*), an astronomer in Flagstaff, Arizona, compared a number of pictures he'd taken over a short period of time of the same area in space. He noticed a faint dot moving in a manner differently than all of the objects around it and realized it must be a planet—Pluto.

And so Pluto became the ninth planet in the Solar System. For more than 75 years it held that spot, until 2006, when the International Astronomical Union—whose opinion is considered very important by scientists—announced that Pluto wasn't a planet after all. Yes, it orbited the Sun. Yes, it was (mostly) round. But, unlike every other planet, it had not knocked out all of the asteroids in its orbit. So Pluto was given a new name—a **dwarf planet**. Pluto is not the only dwarf planet in the Solar System, but it has a

special place because it was considered a "regular" planet for so long.

Pluto doesn't follow the same general path of orbits that the eight primary planets do—the others rotate more or less along the same line, but Pluto's orbit climbs high above and below it. If you think of the planets as revolving like flat circles drawn on a wide

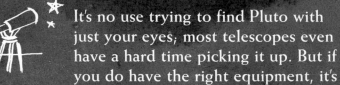

Sky Gazing

It's no use trying to find Pluto with just your eyes; most telescopes even have a hard time picking it up. But if you do have the right equipment, it's recommended that you chart the location of the dwarf planet over a few days. Pluto is so faint that it's hard to tell it apart from surrounding stars, and tracking its movement over several nights is a good way to tell you're on the right spot. The best time to see Pluto is in June.

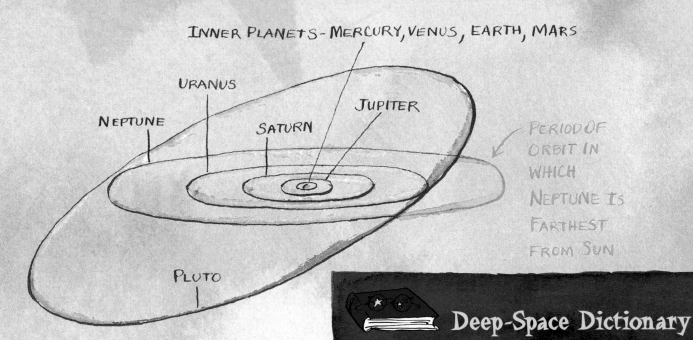

INNER PLANETS—MERCURY, VENUS, EARTH, MARS

NEPTUNE

URANUS

SATURN

JUPITER

PLUTO

PERIOD OF ORBIT IN WHICH NEPTUNE IS FARTHEST FROM SUN

floor with the Sun in the center, Pluto's orbit would sometimes dip below the floor into the basement, or high above into the second story. And, unlike the gassy planets nearby, Pluto is rocky with a real surface you could stand on. (You'd want to bring along a jacket and an oxygen tank, though: The temperature averages several hundred degrees below freezing, and the atmosphere is thought to be mostly methane and nitrogen.) Pluto even has its own moon.

Pluto itself is only about two-thirds the size of the Earth's Moon. But unlike the Moon, Pluto has its own faint atmosphere—or at least, sometimes it does. Pluto is so cold that its atmosphere only appears when Pluto is close to the Sun and the Sun's heat causes some of the ice on Pluto's surface to turn to gas.

Pluto's moon, Charon (*KARE-on*), is unusual in that it orbits so close to Pluto. That's why, from Pluto's surface, Charon would look awfully big in the sky—eighteen times bigger than our Moon appears from Earth. Pluto's moon is also a fast mover, traveling across the sky at four times the speed that the Moon travels across our sky.

Deep-Space Dictionary

dwarf planet A body that orbits a star, is mostly round, but hasn't cleared all of the objects out of its orbital path.

Naming Pluto

When Pluto was discovered, astronomers held an international contest to come up with a name for it. The winner was an 11-year-old girl from England. She suggested naming the new object in the sky after the Roman god of the underworld. The judges thought that was just right for a mysterious planet—or, later, dwarf planet—like Pluto.

NAME:

Pluto

Halley's Comet

HUNKS, CHUNKS
and Flying Objects

Stars and planets get most of the attention when we're talking about space. But there's lots of other cool stuff up there, too. If you plan ahead and bring the right tools, you might even be able to spot one of them!

Asteroids

Asteroids are small chunks of rock and metal floating through space. Almost 5,000 have been spotted between the planets Mars and Jupiter. Some of these asteroids are no bigger than a small stone that you might find in the park. But they can get pretty big, too—at least one asteroid has been found that measures more than 500 miles across!

Some astronomers think that, when the Solar System was first forming, these chunks were kept from coming together and forming another planet because of the pull from the gravity of Jupiter and Mars. If they're right, that means we might have had *ten* planets in the Solar System, rather than nine.

Close-up view of a comet

But not all astronomers think the same way. Some believe that the asteroids between Mars and Jupiter, and others throughout the Solar System, are the remains of a planet that was shattered into pieces by some sort of **cosmic** collision. This is another one of those mysteries of space that has yet to be solved.

Some people blame an asteroid for the death of the dinosaurs 65 million years ago. As the **theory** goes, a giant asteroid crashed into the Earth, setting off a huge explosion. The dinosaurs that weren't immediately killed died later. It is thought that a cloud descended over the whole planet after the asteroid exploded into the Earth, changing the weather and making life impossible not just for dinosaurs, but for many other plants and animals.

Many people wonder what would happen if a giant asteroid were to strike the Earth today. (You might have seen movies or TV programs where something terrible like that happens.) While astronomers can't guarantee that this won't ever happen, they're always keeping an eye on asteroids that pass near the Earth, and don't expect any big ones anytime soon—at least none like the one that might have taken out the dinosaurs.

Asteroids are pretty hard to find in the night sky, because even the big ones are usually too far away to see. But there are other things you *can* look for besides just stars and planets. **Meteors**, for example.

Meteors

When an asteroid or other floating space object comes close enough to the Earth, the planet's gravity pulls it toward the ground. As they plunge earthward, these falling objects are known as meteors. (They are also sometimes called "shooting stars," though they aren't really stars at all.) You can often see a meteor's fiery trail streaking across the sky as the meteor speeds toward the ground. Although we can't see the air that makes up the Earth's atmosphere, we know it's there—it rubs against the side of the speeding meteor fast enough to set it on fire, sort of like when you strike a match against a matchbook.

YEARLY METEOR SHOWERS: AN ANNUAL SHOW

NAME	APPROXIMATE DATE	METEORS PER HOUR (average)
Quadrantids	January 3	50
Perseids	August 12	50
Geminids	December 14	50
Eta Aquarids	May 5	40
Delta Aquarids	July 29	20
Orionids	October 21	20
Ursids	December 22	12

Deep-Space Dictionary

asteroid Small chunks of rock and metal that float through space like mini-planets.

cosmic Having to do with the cosmos (or the universe).

theory An idea or "educated guess" put forth by a scientist to explain something. Scientists test their theories as best they can with hopes of proving them.

meteor A falling object from space that leaves a trail of fire in the sky as it plunges toward the ground. These are often called "shooting stars" or "falling stars" because that's what they look like—but they are actually not stars.

meteorite A meteor that does not burn up in the atmosphere and hits the Earth's surface.

meteor shower A period when the Earth passes through an area of space with lots of floating rocks and other objects. The result is that an unusually high number of meteors often can be seen.

comet A ball of ice and rock hurtling through space in orbit around the Sun. A "tail" appears on a comet when it is close to the Sun.

Often, meteors burn up before ever making it to the ground. When a meteor actually hits the Earth's surface, it gets a different name: a **meteorite**. Astronomers have found meteorites all over the planet. Because they come from places other than Earth, astronomers study them to find out what other stuff in the universe might be made of.

When meteorites hit the ground, they can leave a big hole. Most meteorites weigh only about two pounds, but bigger ones have left craters nearly a mile wide and hundreds of feet deep. (No need to get nervous, though—meteorites this size are very rare.)

The atmosphere of planets like Earth make it tough for meteors to make it to their surfaces, and most burn up before they get here. But meteors have an easier trip down in places with no atmosphere, like Mercury and the Moon, or thin atmospheres, like that of Mars. That's why those places are dotted with so many craters—from all those meteors that became meteorites when they crashed into the surface.

Comets

Meteors are fun to spot, but they're not quite as cool as another special sight in the sky: **comets**.

A comet is a great chunk of ice and rock flying through space at an incredible speed, like a big dirty snowball. Their cores can be anywhere from

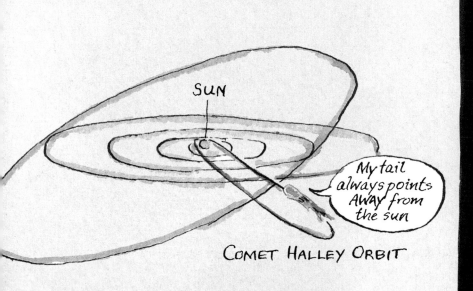

SUN

My tail always points AWAY from the sun

COMET HALLEY ORBIT

Astronomy All-Stars

The most famous comet was named after **Edmond Halley** (pronounced *HAY-lee*), an astronomer who lived from 1656 to 1742. By checking records of appearances of a mysterious light in the sky in 1531, 1607 and 1682, Halley noticed that the sightings happened about every 76 years.

This got him thinking that maybe the comet was in a wide orbit around the Sun, one that brought it near the Earth once every 76 years. If he'd lived to see it, Halley would have no doubt been delighted when the comet reappeared at the end of 1758, just as he'd said it would. It's been known ever since as Halley's Comet.

2 or 3 to 150 miles wide. Comets revolve around the Sun like planets do, and as they approach it, some of their core turns into a gas that forms a long, glowing tail. It's the tail that makes the comet look so spectacular, and it can stretch for hundreds of millions of miles. Sometimes a comet shines so brightly that it can be seen even in broad daylight.

Today we know what comets are, but they mystified earlier viewers. They often thought comets were signs that something particularly good or especially bad was about to happen. Some have even suggested that the star that led the three wise men to Jesus, as the story in the Bible goes, was in fact a comet.

COMET ANATOMY

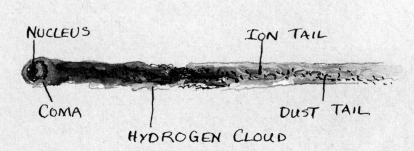

NUCLEUS

COMA

HYDROGEN CLOUD

ION TAIL

DUST TAIL

DOG ANATOMY

BRAIN

KIBBLE

DUSTY TAIL

ION TAIL

CLOUD OF SHED FUR

GALAXIES
Where Stars Hang Out

Spiral Galaxy

When you cast your eyes skyward on a clear night, it might look like the stars are scattered randomly across the sky, like a fistful of glowing marbles that someone tossed into the heavens. But in fact, each star is part of a larger collection of stars that are held together by their gravitational attraction: a **galaxy**.

Some galaxies are so big that, even going in the fastest spaceship ever built, it would take millions of years to get from one side to the other. The galaxy we live in is known as the Milky Way.

Every galaxy is different, but there are three main types:

Elliptical—Elliptical galaxies are named after an ellipse, that misshapen circle we learned about earlier. Elliptical galaxies are round, but longer in one direction than the other. Most of the galaxies in the universe are elliptical.

Spiral—Flat, round clusters of stars with tails that spiral out of a thick, dense center are called spiral galaxies. This is the second-most common type of galaxy.

Irregular—Irregular galaxies have no clear, organized shape. Astronomers believe irregular galaxies are the result of two galaxies bumping into each other, or one galaxy being stretched into a strange shape by the pull of another one nearby.

Deep-Space Dictionary

★★★★★★★★★★★★★★★★★★★★★★★★★★★★★★★★★

galaxy A great collection of stars held together by gravity.

Astronomers believe that there are at least 50 billion galaxies in the universe. If each galaxy contains billions, maybe *trillions*, of stars, that means there are more stars in the universe than there are grains of sand on all the beaches in the world.

A Galaxy of Our Own: The Milky Way

Our home, the Milky Way, is one galaxy that you can see using only your eyes. Just about every object you see in the night sky is part of it.

Think of the Milky Way, a spiral galaxy, as round and flat, sort of like a giant Frisbee. It has a big lump in the middle and edges that spiral off like a pinwheel. Our Sun, and the rest of the Solar System, is near the edge of the galaxy. But even from our home near the Milky Way's border, the galaxy's closest edge is still millions of miles away. Altogether, the Milky Way is about 100,000 light-years across at its widest point. At its thick center, it is about 15,000 light-years from top to bottom.

You might wonder why they would name a galaxy after something you'd find in a candy store, but the

Sky Gazing

On the clearest of clear nights, if you're far from the bright lights of the city, you may be able to spot a wide, hazy strip stretching all the way across the sky. That's part of the Milky Way! That haze is caused by the combined light of the billions of stars that make up the galaxy. That strip is a side view of the galaxy. It stretches for thousands of light-years off into the distance.

truth is the other way around—the galaxy was named "milky" long before the chocolate bar. The whitish strip in the sky reminded early star gazers of a stream of spilt milk, although others have given it different names. Egyptians once called it the Road of Souls. Some African tribes knew it as the Backbone of Night.

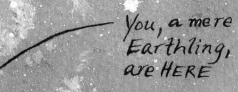

You, a mere Earthling, are HERE

An elliptical galaxy

An irregular galaxy

What We Can't See
(but we think is there)

COSMIC MYSTERIES

The universe is filled with mysteries, things that scientists are only half sure of, things they argue about amongst themselves—even things they don't understand at all. One of the most fascinating mysteries is how the universe began. One popular explantion is the **Big Bang theory**, the idea that everything we know of came into being as a result of one big explosion some 15 billion years ago. Another mystery is gravity.

Gravity

We all know what gravity does—it's the force that pulls one object toward another. Every object has its own gravity that pulls on other objects. How strong that pull is depends on how massive the object is, and how close it is to the objects it is pulling in.

The dense core at the center of the Earth pulls things toward it, which is what keeps us from floating off the surface and up into space. The Sun's gravity keeps the planets in the Solar System revolving around it. And the combined gravity of numerous stars pulling on one another leads them to band together into galaxies like our very own Milky Way. What we *don't* know is exactly how or why gravity works. That's a mystery for future generations to solve.

One interesting way to think of gravity is to imagine the universe as a large rubber sheet stretched tight above the floor. If you were to place a golf ball on it, the rubber would sink a bit around the ball, and anything else on the sheet would tend to slide or roll toward it. A heavier item, like a baseball, would pull the sheet down even more, and draw things in

GRAVITY LOSS—COULD IT HAPPEN TO YOU?

BEFORE   AFTER

BEFORE   AFTER

Astronomy All-Stars

Gravity is the force that makes you fall on the floor, rather than the ceiling, when you trip over something. In the seventeenth century, legend has it that the scientist **Sir Isaac Newton** figured out  gravity when he was hit on the head by a falling apple. He came up with the idea that objects (like the Earth) naturally pull other objects toward them (like the apple that bonked him on the head on the way down). The concept of gravity has become accepted as one of the most important laws of science.

study other things. For example, astronomers observing spiral galaxies have wondered why some of the stars don't drift off. They know that there is a dense core at the center of the galaxy, but there doesn't appear to be enough stuff there to create gravity strong enough to keep all of those stars together. That has led some astronomers to think that there must be some "dark matter" that we can't see and don't really understand that's helping to hold everything together.

What is dark matter, how did it get there and what does it do? We can't answer any of these questions yet. But most astronomers think that it's out there, and that it is a very important part of our universe.

SMALL BALL

BIG BALL

toward it more strongly. The universe seems to work in much the same way—dense, heavy items like stars and black holes pull things toward them strongly. Even small items have the power to pull other things. The apple that Newton saw falling to the Earth was pulling the Earth up toward it just a tiny bit.

Dark Matter

Astronomers are smart, but, as we've learned, they don't understand everything.

But, even when they don't completely understand something, they can use their partial knowledge to

Black Holes

Another one of the great mysteries astronomers are only beginning to understand is the **black hole**.

We learned earlier about how stars burn off their energy toward the end of their lives. But not all stars just fade away after shrinking into black dwarves or exploding into supernovas. Some especially big stars get smaller and smaller and denser and denser until they eventually become powerful pits tinier than the head of a pin. These objects—black holes—have gravity so strong that they suck in everything around them, and even light can't escape their gravity. (That's why we call them "black.")

Honey, I wouldn't get too close...

53

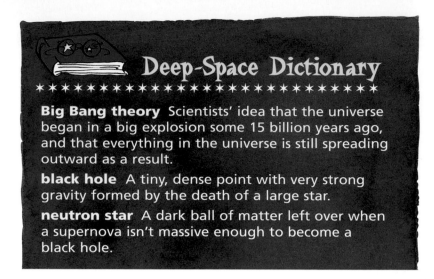
Big Bang theory Scientists' idea that the universe began in a big explosion some 15 billion years ago, and that everything in the universe is still spreading outward as a result.

black hole A tiny, dense point with very strong gravity formed by the death of a large star.

neutron star A dark ball of matter left over when a supernova isn't massive enough to become a black hole.

Many astronomers believe that at the center of some galaxies—including the Milky Way—these great, dense, dark areas exist. There, a black hole sucks in nearby objects and holds the surrounding stars in its orbit by the force of gravity. Although most agree that black holes exist, no one understands quite how they work, or exactly what happens to the stars and other objects that are sucked inside them.

And there's one big problem with trying to study black holes: Because their gravity is so strong, they pull in *everything*—including light and the other forms of energy astronomers normally study to learn about objects in the sky. As a result, astronomers must examine other objects in the area where they think a black hole might be. Then the astronomers work backward, using what they know about these other objects to figure out how a black hole nearby might be affecting them.

... and a New ("Neu") Puzzle

Exploding stars that aren't dense enough to become black holes become **neutron stars**. They don't have a black hole's power to suck things in, but, like black holes, they don't have the energy to give out light. Instead, neutron stars send out energy in ways that we can detect only by using special instruments. And astronomers can't say they've ever really seen a neutron star.

Exploring What's Up There

We've already learned about some of the brilliant people—like Copernicus, Sir Isaac Newton and Edmond Halley—who spent their time scanning the skies, thinking about and discovering many of the things that we take for granted today. Along with them, a lot of astronomers and some very brave space travelers called astronauts have explored the universe. In this section, you'll learn about the tools they created to help them explore. You'll also find out how you can be an astronomer, too, with the help of your eyes, some simple tools and the Star Finder in this book. You'll learn how to find and recognize stars, constellations, planets and other objects in the night sky—right from your own backyard.

What Astronauts and Astronomers Do

There are plenty of cool things that you can see in the night sky with just your own two eyes, if you know how to spot them. You can see the Moon, stars, planets, meteors, sometimes even comets.

GALILEO'S TELESCOPE

Tools for Star Gazers

To really get a good look at everything, it helps to have extra tools. Galileo perfected the early **telescope**, and since then, other astronomers have improved upon it greatly. Galileo's first telescope made things appear closer by using lenses sort of like those you'd find in a magnifying glass. It could be held in one hand, and it made things appear eight times closer than they actually were. Today, telescopes that you can buy and use at home magnify objects hundreds of times. Some of the special telescopes that mainly professional astronomers use are so big that whole buildings have to be constructed just to hold them.

Lots of people own hand-held magnifiers called **binoculars**. Your parents might have a pair that they take to the ballgame or the opera. They're also great tools for looking at stars. Binoculars are really just two telescopes placed side by side, one for each eye, and are particularly good for gazing at clusters of stars, like the Pleiades (which we'll learn about on page 74).

BINOCULARS

Those buildings that house the biggest telescopes are called **observatories**, because that's where people go to *observe* the heavens. But people have been building observatories for centuries, even back before we had telescopes. The first ones were built in Greece and the Middle East thousands of years ago. The ancient observatories often had tall walls or towers that people could climb in order to get a clear view of the sky with nothing in the way. Back then, many people believed that the stars were magical and could help predict the future, so priests and other religious leaders used these old-fashioned observatories as much as early astronomers did.

There's another kind of big telescope, too, that isn't housed in an observatory. It's out in space! The Hubble Space Telescope is a remarkable telescope

Astronomy All-Stars

Galileo Galilei was an Italian astronomer who lived from 1564 to 1642, around the same time as William Shakespeare, back when Europeans were just beginning to explore America. The idea that the Earth was round was still pretty new for some people, and many still insisted that the Earth was the center of the universe—but Galileo knew better, and he needed the tools to prove what he believed.

Galileo is known as the inventor of the telescope, even though his wasn't the first—it was just the best one anyone had yet built. Using his telescopes, Galileo made observations that he felt proved that the planets revolved around the Sun. But people still wouldn't believe it. He was brought to court by church leaders and forced to say that the Earth was, indeed, the center of the universe—although he knew that was wrong.

Edwin Hubble was a twentieth-century astronomer who helped us understand how the universe works. By studying the distances between galaxies, Hubble found that galaxies are constantly moving away from one another.

Hubble's important discovery led to a scientific idea known as the Big Bang theory, which says that the universe began about 15 billion years ago with a huge explosion that sent energy flying out in all directions—and eventually led to the stars, planets and everything else in the universe.

To understand how the Big Bang theory works, think about the universe as a half-inflated balloon with dots on the outside representing galaxies. As you blow up the balloon, the dots, or galaxies, get farther apart. Believers in the Big Bang theory say that this is just how the universe works—always expanding, with everything in it slowly spreading farther and farther out.

that was put into orbit around the Earth in 1990. From high above the Earth's surface, it has a clear view of the universe— much clearer than telescopes on Earth, which have to peer through the atmosphere before they can spot something in space. Named after Edwin Hubble, the Hubble Space Telescope can make things appear 6,000 times closer than they

HUBBLE TELESCOPE

are, and has spotted galaxies more than 58 sextillion miles away. (That's 58 with twenty-one zeroes after it!) Then it sends pictures of what it sees back to us on Earth. These are the best pictures we've ever had of some *very* faraway places.

HUBBLE TELESCOPE

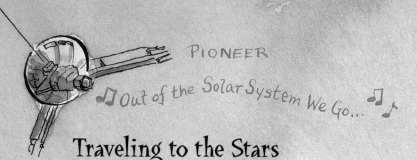

PIONEER

♪ Out of the Solar System We Go... ♪♪

"Tanks moving to Southeast..."

SPY SATELLITE

Traveling to the Stars

People have dreamed of traveling into space for centuries, but it has taken us a long time to get there.

Gravity is the hard part. As we've learned, the force of the Earth's gravity pulls things toward the ground, so scientists first had to figure out how to overcome that force to make it beyond the Earth's pull and out into space. That's where the **rocket** comes in. Rockets leave Earth with so much force that they overcome its gravitational pull. As a rocket burns its fuel, it sends gas out in one direction. That causes the rocket to travel in the opposite direction—fast.

After several experiments and many years, the Russians were the first to use a rocket to put a ship into space. They launched *Sputnik 1* on October 4, 1957, and it orbited the Earth in a little over an hour-and-a-half. As it did, it sent back information to astronomers on the ground through radio waves.

"Operator? Operator ?!!"

TELEPHONE SATELLITE

Since then, astronomers have sent many more **satellites** into space. These objects orbit the Earth and send information back to the planet, just like *Sputnik 1* did. Some satellites take pictures, some beam phone calls and television programs back and forth across the globe and others collect weather **data** (a scientific word for "information"). Some military satellites are even equipped with lasers designed to shoot down missiles during a war.

Astronomers have also sent many unmanned spacecraft, or **probes**, on one-way trips far into the Solar System and beyond. (While satellites revolve around a planet or other object, a probe zooms off into space, never to return.) Probes are loaded with cameras and other equipment to study the planets and other objects they encounter. And probes have special communicators that allow them to send data across millions of miles back to the Earth.

♪ Neptune .

The *Mariner* probes, launched in the 1960s and '70s, traveled to Mercury, Venus and Mars. They didn't land on the planets (although later probes would make it to the surface of Mars

♪♪ Mercury... Venus... Mars
It's oh so far(s) ♪♪ ♪

MARINER

WEATHER SATELLITE

"Rain tomorrow, clearing toward afternoon"

and Venus), but they got close enough to teach us much of what we know today about the planets nearest the Sun.

The *Pioneer* probes went in the opposite direction, away from the Sun, and made visits past Jupiter and Saturn before heading out of the Solar System altogether. The *Voyager* probes collected data from Neptune and Uranus before heading for uncharted territories in outer space. Once they completed their missions, the *Pioneer* probes just kept going, and now they have traveled too far away for their instruments to communicate with Earth. But the *Voyager* probes still check in every day with scientists back home, sending their latest findings.

...anus... Off to the unknown(us) ♪♫

VOYAGER

"Do you really love me?"

TELEVISION SATELLITE

Astronomy All-Stars

Robert Goddard, an American scientist, launched the first modern rocket in 1926. His rocket didn't make it into space, but it was still quite a breakthrough. Rather than using solid fuel, Goddard's rocket used liquid fuel, which provided more power but was lighter weight, so it didn't weigh the rocket down. This new kind of fuel would be used later to launch satellites—and then people—into space.

Deep-Space Dictionary

★ ★

telescope A special instrument (usually in the shape of a tube) that uses lenses and sometimes mirrors to make faraway objects appear closer.

binoculars A portable magnifying device for viewing distant objects that consists of two little telescopes side by side, one for each eye.

observatory A laboratory, often high on a mountain, where scientists use telescopes and other tools to study the stars. Ancient observatories were simply places that got you closer to the heavens, or offered a better look at them.

rocket A spaceship that uses the gas released by burning fuel to achieve incredibly high speeds (enough to escape the Earth's gravity).

satellite A spacecraft launched into orbit around the Earth or other heavenly body. (Technically, anything that orbits a planet or star is considered a satellite, including a moon.)

data Scientific information.

probe A spacecraft launched from Earth and sent to collect information from distant places like other planets, asteroids or moons.

Astronauts with Fur

Although humans have long dreamed of traveling to the stars, we weren't the first creatures to make it into space—monkeys and dogs beat us to it.

Ham, the first chimp to orbit the Earth.

A Russian dog named Laika and a chimpanzee named Ham were among a handful of animals that were sent into orbit around the Earth aboard rockets in the 1950s and '60s. They proved that life could indeed survive in space, and helped pave the way for the humans who would follow them.

On April 21, 1961, less than four years after the Russians first launched *Sputnik 1*, they sent a man into space for almost two hours before bringing him back safely to the Earth. Yuri Gagarin (*YUR-ee guh-GARE-in*) was the first **cosmonaut**—the Russian word for astronaut, or someone who travels into space.

For a time, the Russians led the Americans in the **Space Race**, an unofficial contest to see whose space program could achieve the greatest feats and make the most important discoveries. But on July 20, 1969, American astronaut Neil Armstrong became the first man to step on the surface of the Moon. This had been one of the main goals of both countries' space programs. The United States has led the way into space ever since.

The spaceships you're probably most familiar with are the **Space Shuttles**. These ships were unlike the rockets that had been used before. Those rockets could be used only once—they would blast off, drop fuel tanks and other pieces once they were done with them, then return to Earth as just a tiny capsule big enough to hold a few astronauts.

The Space Shuttles are different. they look like a cross between an airplane and a rocket. First

THE REAL SPUTNIK

beep, beep!

HALLOWEEN SPUTNIK

beep, beep!

Tapered paper cones

Rice paper globe painted silver

Discard fuel tank

Low earth orbit

Research and work

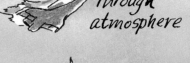
In position for return

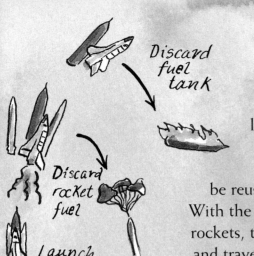
Discard rocket fuel

Launch

Through atmosphere

Landing

launched in 1981, the Shuttles were the first spacecraft designed to be reused again and again. With the help of their booster rockets, they can blast off upright and travel through space, then land back on Earth like a plane. But unlike an airplane, the Space Shuttle's powerful engine gives it enough power to fly out of the Earth's atmosphere.

The Shuttles are built to carry eight to ten astronauts and can stay in space for more than a week. They have been used for a variety of things, including conducting space experiments, repairing the Hubble telescope and carrying the parts for a space station—a floating city in space.

A City in Space

If life on Earth bores you and you think you'd prefer to spend your days somewhere else in space, you're not completely out of luck. We haven't found any planets yet that humans could live on, but we have built some cities of our own up in the sky. You might want to consider a space station.

Space stations are like tiny towns in space. They orbit the Earth and are built as homes for astronauts spending long periods up there. The Soviets sent up the first space station in 1971, and cosmonauts lived in it for 22 days.

In May 1973, the Americans followed with their own space station, Skylab. Three-person crews took turns manning the station, and some stayed aboard it for as long as 84 days—a record at the time.

The space stations have allowed astronomers to study the Sun, the Earth, the planets and many other things. Today, scientists from sixteen different countries use the International Space Station, an ever-expanding outpost floating high above the Earth, to study the mysteries of the universe, and to conduct experiments that, because of the planet's gravity, they could not perform on Earth.

Although the Space Race isn't as hotly contested as it once was, astronomers are making new advances in space exploration every day. In 2003, the Chinese launched their first astronauts into orbit in a satellite similar to the ships the Russians used to send cosmonauts into space more than 40 years earlier.

Deep-Space Dictionary
★★★★★★★★★★★★★★★★★★★★★★★★★★★

astronaut A person who travels into space. Russians call their space travelers **cosmonauts**.

Space Race An unofficial contest that developed between the United States and the Soviet Union in the mid-twentieth century to see who could first place a rocket in orbit, send a human into space, land a man on the moon and achieve other great space feats.

Space Shuttle An American spacecraft that takes off like a rocket and lands like an airplane, and can be used many times.

Astronomers have all kinds of plans when asked what the future may hold. For years they have talked about sending humans to land on Mars much the way they landed on the Moon. And, speaking of the Moon, the Chinese are hoping to send their astronauts there before the year 2010. There's also been talk of a permanent settlement on the Moon. (There's another option for folks who think the Earth is just too boring.) And astronomers have other big plans. For one, they're sending more probes to investigate the Solar System—one group hopes to land a probe on Saturn's moon, Titan.

We learned earlier that there are trillions and trillions of stars out there in space—and there might be just as many possibilities for exploring them.

Alone in the Universe?

You've probably read books with wild tales about little green men from the planet Mars, or seen movies featuring strange-looking characters from faraway planets visiting Earth.

But extraterrestrial life—or life beyond the planet Earth—is not just a subject for science-fiction writers and Hollywood moviemakers. Some very smart scientists and astronomers have also wondered what forms of life might exist in the deep reaches of space.

When the *Voyager* probes were launched in 1977, they were sent with greetings from Earth, just in case any aliens ever came across them as the probes made their long, lonely journeys through the universe. Gold-plated discs—complete with their own machines that could play both sounds and images—featured greetings in 55 languages, pictures of life on Earth and information about where the probes came from. Some of the most brilliant scientists from around the world came together to create these glimpses of life on Earth.

Although no one has proof that life exists elsewhere in the universe, many scientists think there's a pretty good chance of it. We know there are billions and billions of stars, and that our Sun is a fairly typical one. We also know that there are planets orbiting other stars—scientists' best guess is that planets are actually pretty common. With all those stars and all those planets, it's only logical that another planet with some kind of life on it exists out there somewhere. (As one scientist once put it, "If there's not life out there, it is a terrible waste of space!") That life might be a plant, some sort of animal, or—more likely—a form of life different from anything we know.

Finding that life is another matter. Stars are so far apart that it would take 100,000 years just to get to our closest star, Alpha Centauri, and that's traveling in the fastest spacecraft ever built. We may build faster ships in the future, but most scientists don't think it's possible to build ships that could approach the speed of light. So any trip to visit our neighbors orbiting the next star over would probably take an impossibly long time.

Our best bet for finding extraterrestrial life, then, may just be to listen for it. Because radio waves can travel so fast and so far, scientists figure that intelligent life on other planets might use that method to communicate. Since the 1960s, astronomers have pointed giant radio telescopes toward distant stars, hoping they just might catch a message from an alien. They've begun to look for other signals, too, like laser flashes. So far: nothing. But if we ever do find life out there, most people agree that it would be the biggest discovery in human history. So the search continues....

The Challenge of Space

Movies like *Star Wars* make space travel look easy. Just hop in your star cruiser, rev up the engines and take off. But we all know that sending spacecraft—and especially people—beyond the Earth's orbit is an incredibly difficult task. And a dangerous one.

Deep-Space Dictionary

space station An orbiting satellite that serves as a home for astronauts and scientists to work and live in, like a man-made "city" in space.

The Russian and American space programs have each had accidents in which astronauts lost their lives, including the seven killed when the Space Shuttle *Challenger* exploded just after takeoff on January 28, 1986. Seven more astronauts were killed on February 1, 2003, when the Space Shuttle *Columbia* broke apart because of problems with its heat shield as it reentered the Earth's atmosphere. Researchers learn from their mistakes and use that knowledge to try and make space travel safer. Still, journeying into space remains an exciting, but dangerous, job.

The Space Shuttle <u>Atlantis</u> undocks from the <u>Mir</u> Space Station

WHAT YOU CAN DO

You don't need your own observatory or spaceship to become an astronomer. If you know what to look for and when to look, there's a whole world of fascinating things you can study from your backyard, the park down the street or any other wide-open space. Using your new knowledge about the night sky and your eyes, you can pick out all kinds of cool stuff. And the Star Finder included with this book will help you find some of the most interesting objects in the night sky—the **constellations**.

When the first star gazers stared up at the night sky, they saw shapes in the thousands of stars that dotted the heavens. By imagining lines between the points of light, they grouped the stars together into pictures called constellations.

Today there are eighty-eight accepted constellations, and they include everything from a warrior to a dragon to a river. Some of the best-known constellations are the twelve that form what is known as the **zodiac** (*ZO-dee-ack*). These constellations are lined up in one long band, and from our view, they appear to move steadily across the sky so that all of them pass by us over the course of one year. But we'll learn more about the zodiac later.

Light Pollution

In big cities, the dirty air and the glare of bright lights can make it hard to see stars. But even in dark places, the glare from a flashlight or other light source can force your eyes to adjust to it, which makes the stars appear dim when you look back up at the sky. (It's sort of like when you walk into a dark room after being out in the bright sunlight—it takes a while for your eyes to get used to the darkness.)

When you take the Star Finder or this book out with you when you're looking at stars, try painting the tip of a flashlight with pink or red nail polish before you use it. That will keep the light from being so bright that your eyes have to readjust—but the red glow will still provide enough light for you to read.

Sky Gazing with the Star Finder

Tucked inside the cover of this book is the Star Finder, which will help you when you head out to look at the stars.

Because the Earth rotates in place and revolves around the Sun, the sky above us is constantly in motion. By setting the current date and the correct time, you can use the Star Finder to provide a map of what the sky looks like at any time.

The first thing to do is check your watch or a clock, then find the current hour on the list of hours that runs along the outside of the spinning disc in the middle of the Star Finder.

Then find the current month on the Star Finder's base. If it's early in the month—say, the first week—look to the left portion of that month's section. If it's late in the month, look to the right portion. If you're smack dab in the middle of the month—June 15, for example—look right in the center of the "June" marker.

Now, to set your Star Finder, spin the disc until the hour marker on the disc lines up with the month marker you found on the base. The stars and constellations you see inside the Star Finder's highlighted circle should now match the skies above!

All that's left is to make sure you're facing the right direction. Use a compass or ask a grownup to show you which way is north, then line up the "north" marker on the Star Finder so that it faces the same direction. Now look up!

THE BIG DIPPER and THE GREAT BEAR

Everyone's favorite group of stars—probably because it's one of the easiest to recognize—is the Big Dipper. In many places, including the United States, it can be seen all year 'round. Americans usually describe it as a giant spoon or "dipper," but others peering at this bright collection of stars have seen carts, wagons or even animals.

We learned earlier that there are eighty-eight official constellations, but—surprise—the Big Dipper isn't one of them. In fact, the Big Dipper is part of a larger constellation, the Great Bear, or *Ursa Major* in Latin. The Great Bear is highest in the sky in the summer and lowest in the winter. According to Native American legend, this is because the Bear is looking for a place to hibernate during the cold winter months.

THE LITTLE DIPPER (or the Little Bear)

Just above the Big Dipper's cup you can find the Little Dipper. This constellation is smaller than the Big Dipper (you saw that coming, right?), and is also known as *Ursa Minor*, or the Little Bear. The

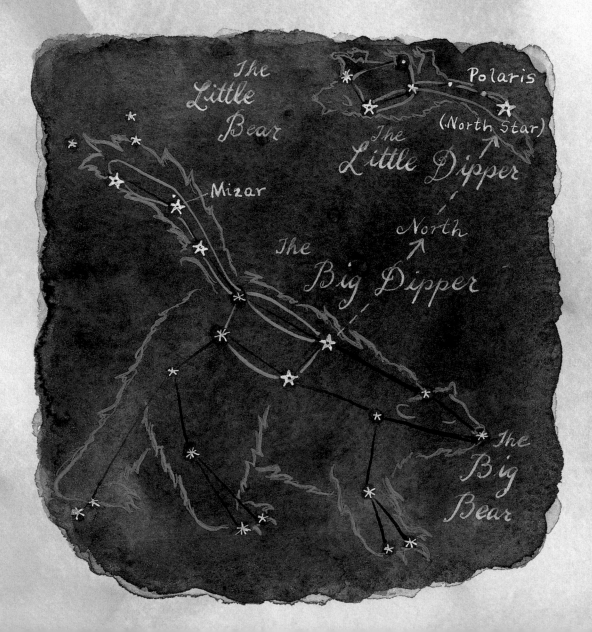

Star Finding

As we said earlier, the Big Dipper is pretty easy to find because it's so big and bright. It can be seen all year long, but is especially visible between January and October. If you set the Star Finder for the month of the year and the time of night when you're searching, it will show you where to look. The Big Dipper is generally found in the northern part of the sky.

If you can find the Big Dipper, you can use it to find the Little Dipper, too. If you draw an imaginary line straight up from the two stars that make up the far end of the Big Dipper's spoon (called the Pointers), you soon come across the bright Pole Star. That's the tip of the Little Bear's tail—or the tip of the Little Dipper's handle, if you prefer.

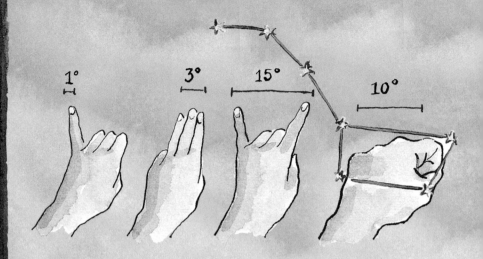

brightest of the Little Dipper's stars is the Pole Star. The Pole star is also known as the North Star or Polaris (*po-LARE-iss*). Any time you're facing it, you can be sure you're looking north. Many people throughout history have found their way by following the Pole Star. You can, too—if you can spot the Pole Star, you can tell which direction you're facing without using a compass.

Mapping the Stars

If you hold your hand up to the sky and place it right where you find the Big Dipper's cup, you'll find that your fist just about fits inside it. Astronomers charting the sky from the Earth measure that distance as about ten **degrees**.

But these aren't like the degrees on a thermometer, which measure how hot or cold something is. Instead, try and imagine the sky as a big, black cloth spread out overhead and the stars as dots scattered across it. The distance across the sky is measured in degrees, and one degree is about the width of your little finger as it's held up to the sky. Three fingers equal about five degrees, and the distance between your pinky and your index finger, extended wide like the horns of a bull, is about fifteen degrees. People's hands are different sizes, so a smaller hand with pinkie and thumb stretched wide will be a little less than fifteen degrees, and a big hand will be a little more. Be sure to keep your hand a full arm's length away and your measurements will be more accurate. Try it out by measuring the distance between the Big Dipper and the Pole Star—that's about twenty-eight degrees.

Deep-Space Dictionary

degree The unit astronomers use to measure the distance between the stars as seen from the Earth.

THE BIG DOG

The Big Dog, or *Canis Major*, looks like he's barking up at Orion, which sounds about right—early astronomers imagined him as Orion's companion. In the neck of the Big Dog is a star called Sirius (*SEER-ious*), Latin for "Dog Star." Sirius is a binary (or double) star, and is the brightest star in the entire night sky. (If you see something brighter, it's probably a planet.)

THE UNICORN

To Orion's left, above the Big Dog, is the Unicorn, the legendary white horse with the dazzling horn jutting out of his forehead. If you can locate that bright star Betelgeuse on Orion's shoulder, you can find the Unicorn's horn next to that. It, too, is best seen around January.

Star Stories

Many of the stories we tell about the constellations come from the **myths** of the ancient Greeks, Romans and other cultures. They weren't the first star gazers, but their stories about gods and heroes are some of the most famous. They've been told and retold for centuries, and some of them are very exciting. Sometimes it is easier to spot the constellations when you remember the stories.

ORION

One of the biggest and most brilliant constellations in the night sky is Orion. He's a soldier standing tall, and wears a belt made up of three bright stars. In addition to his easy-to-find waist, the supergiant star called Betelgeuse (*BEETLE-juice*) can be found on his shoulder. ("Betelgeuse" is Arabic for "shoulder of the giant.") Another bright star, Rigel (*RYE-gel*), makes up his right knee. Orion is carrying his weapons into battle. Greek legend has it that he's a lonely wanderer searching for love.

68

Measuring the Stars

Orion and the Big Dog contain some of the brightest stars in the sky. Every star is different when it comes to brightness, and one of the ways astronomers measure this difference is through **magnitude**. A star's magnitude is a measure of how brightly it shines in the sky. The magnitude scale ranges from 6.0 (the very faintest stars) to 0.0 (the very brightest stars). Some things are even brighter, however—like the Sun and the Moon. These objects go past zero into the negative scale. The Moon's magnitude is -12.6, and the Sun's is -26.8.

But just because one star has a higher magnitude than another doesn't mean it's actually giving off more light. Stars that are closer to us appear brighter than those that are farther away.

So astronomers have divided "magnitude" into two kinds. Apparent magnitude measures how bright a star appears to be from the Earth. Absolute magnitude measures how much light a star is actually giving off. (The measurements above for the brightness of the Sun and the Moon are their apparent magnitudes.)

Deep-Space Dictionary

myth A legend or tale from an ancient culture, often featuring gods interacting with mortals. Some of these myths are used to describe the pictures we see when we look at the constellations.

magnitude A scientific measurement of the brightness of a star, ranging from 6.0 (faintest) to 0.0 (brightest). Apparent magnitude measures how bright a star appears to be when seen from the Earth. Absolute magnitude measures how much light a star is really giving off.

THE TEN BRIGHTEST STARS IN THE NIGHT SKY

STAR	APPARENT MAGNITUDE	ABSOLUTE MAGNITUDE	DISTANCE FROM THE EARTH (in light-years)
Sirius	-1.46	1.4	8.5
Canopus	-0.72	-2.5	316.
Alpha Centauri	-0.29	4.1	4.28
Arcturus	-0.04	0.2	36.
Vega	0.04	0.6	25.
Capella	0.08	0.4	42.
Rigel	0.11	-8.1	775.
Procyon	0.37	2.6	11.4
Achernar	0.46	-1.3	144.
Betelgeuse	0.5	-7.2	430.

Star Finding

The best time to find Orion, the Big Dog and the Unicorn is during the winter months, especially around January. If you check for them on the Star Finder, you'll see that they are found most often in the southern sky, not far above the horizon. The Big Dog is lowest in the sky, and appears to be looking up at his master, Orion. The Unicorn is above the Big Dog, and also faces Orion just to the warrior's left.

PEGASUS

We've learned already that we can look at stars in many ways—while some people have seen a large spoon when they looked at what we know as the Big Dipper, others have seen a wagon with reins that would be fastened to a horse. Even when people agree on the object a constellation represents, they sometimes still see it different ways.

The winged horse Pegasus is a good example. Most star gazers agree that three of the four stars that form what is known as the Great Square make up its wing. But some imagine the full outline of the animal in the sky, while others see only half a horse. Who's to say who's right? There are billions of pairs of eyes on the Earth, and even more stars in the sky. And there are just as many ways to see them.

According to Greek mythology, the owner of Pegasus, a man named Bellerophon (*ba-LARE-a-fon*), tried to fly the horse into the heavens—but the gods would not allow a human in, so Bellerophon fell from the horse's back. That's why we see the outline of the winged horse flying solo in the sky.

ANDROMEDA

In the outline many astronomers use, three stars of the Great Square make up the wing of Pegasus. The fourth is linked to another constellation—Andromeda (*ann-DRAH-mi-duh*). That fourth star of the Great Square, Alpheratz (*al-FEE-rats*), makes up the goddess' head, and the rest of the constellation is pictured as a woman stretched out in the sky. On an especially clear night you might just be able to make out a hazy spot to her right—that's the Andromeda Galaxy. Of all the objects in the sky that can be seen with just your eyes, this galaxy is the farthest thing from the Earth—about 2.7 million light-years away.

The Greek myth goes that Andromeda's mother boasted so much about her daughter's beauty that she angered a group of sea goddesses. They sent a monster to destroy Andromeda's homeland, and her parents offered their beautiful daughter as a sacrifice. But just before the monster devoured her, a hero named Perseus (*PUR-see-us*) heard Andromeda's cries and rescued her. The two of them then escaped on Pegasus' back.

North

Andromeda
Galaxy

Andromeda

Alpheratz

Deneb

To
Cygnus

Great
Square

Pegasus

Markab

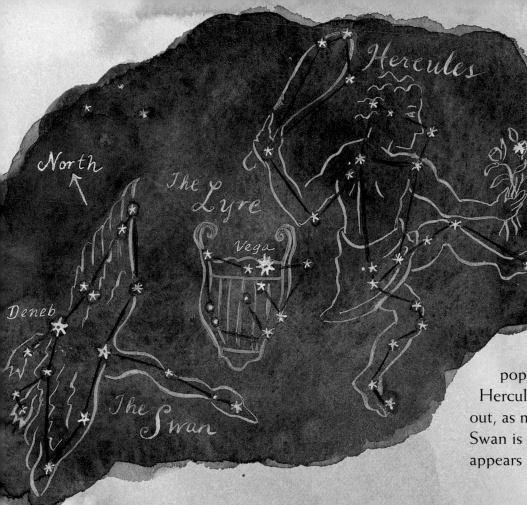

and turned him into a beautiful, white bird flying forever in the night sky.

HERCULES

Hercules (*HER-cue-leez*) is one of the bigger constellations, which makes sense because it is named after one of the strongest and bravest heroes of Greek legend. He pops up again and again in their stories. But Hercules is not the easiest constellation to make out, as many of his stars are faint. The head of the Swan is pointed toward Hercules' left foot, and he appears to be raising a great club into the sky.

THE SWAN

Cygnus (*SIG-nus*) is another name for the Swan (sometimes called the Northern Cross). This big, brilliant group of stars (not an official constellation) contains two rows of stars that cross like a giant "Γ." Just above the swan's neck is Vega, one of the five brightest stars in the sky.

The Romans once believed that the god Zeus changed himself into a swan in order to win the heart of a beautiful woman named Leda. The Greeks, on the other hand, believed that the Swan was once a man who had become so heartbroken when his friend died that the gods took pity on him

Star Finding

The best time to look for Pegasus, Andromeda, the Swan and Hercules is between late summer and fall. Look for the Great Square on the Star Finder, then see if you can spot it in the sky. That's the wing of Pegasus, and the flying horse looks like he is galloping up toward the Pole Star. The highest star of the Great Square marks the head of Andromeda. She seems to be stretched out across the sky with her feet pointing toward the northern horizon. The Swan lies to the west of Pegasus, and appears to be flying away from Andromeda. Its beak points toward Hercules' left foot, and Hercules is about to bring his club crashing down toward the ground.

THE ZODIAC ZOO

Of the eighty-eight constellations in the sky, twelve are particularly special—they are the zodiac constellations we learned about earlier. They're not all easy to find, but they are important to know about, as they mark the places in the sky where we look for the other planets in the Solar System.

The first astronomers noticed that as the Sun and the visible planets moved across the sky, they seemed to travel along a set course, passing through a narrow belt of stars and never venturing outside of it. (Of course, you can't see the constellations behind the Sun, because it outshines every star in the sky. But if you could, you'd see that it follows along this path, too.) This course is called the **ecliptic** (*e-CLIP-tic*).

The constellations in that band became known as the constellations of the zodiac. These constellations wrap around the Earth like a giant belt. On any given night, five or six of the zodiac constellations may be visible, lined up one after another in order. "Zodiac" is a Greek word for "belt of living things." In the sky, the zodiac includes twelve constellations named after people, symbols and animals.

About 4,000 years ago, star gazers came to believe that the positions of the stars and planets in the sky actually controlled or predicted things that happened on Earth. They believed, for example, that because Mars was red, it was linked to war and anger. Its appearance in the sky could mean that a great battle was about to take place.

The constellations were also thought to have power over Earthly events. For example, one particular constellation often appeared in the sky during the time of year when rains were heavy. People began to associate that constellation with stormy weather, and they soon started to see in it the image of someone pouring a bucket of water. They named this constellation Aquarius, the Water Carrier. (We'll learn more about Aquarius later.)

cheerful, proud, powerful

Leo The Lion
July 23–Aug.22

modest, practical, tidy

Virgo
The Virgin Aug.

bold, courageous, energetic

Aries
The Ram March 21–
April 19

conservative, stubborn, loyal

Taurus
The Bull April 20–
May 20

lively, talkative, intelligent

blah, blah
$E = mc^2$

Gemini
The Twins May 21–
June 20

thoughtful, patriotic, emotional

Cancer
The Crab
June 21–July 22

secretive, passionate, intense

Scorpio
The Scorpion
Oct. 23 – Nov. 21

happy, generous, restless

Sagittarius
The Archer
Nov. 22 – Dec. 21

ambitious, cautious, practical

Capricorn
The Goat
Dec. 22 – Jan 19

curious, outgoing, independent

Aquarius
The Water Carrier
Jan. 20 – Feb. 18

artistic, caring, sensitive

Pisces
The Fishes
Feb. 19 – Mar. 20

cooperative, nice

Libra
The Scales
Sept. 23 – Oct. 22

Each of the twelve constellations in the zodiac represents a time of year roughly a month long. For many years the Greeks thought (and some people still believe) that a person's personality is affected by the constellation, or "sign," that the Sun was passing through at the time of his or her birthday. (If you were born in early March, for example, you were born under the sign of Pisces, the Fishes.)

The study of zodiac birth signs is called **astrology**. Astrology may seem silly, but for centuries it was considered as real as any scientific fact. Today, millions of people check the newspaper every day to read their **horoscopes**—predictions of what the day may have in store for them based on their astrological signs. Some read them just for fun, but others swear that there's truth in astrology. Either way, we have early astrologers to thank for much of what we know about the stars. The study of the zodiac signs and their effects on our lives isn't exactly a science, but because it involves the stars, it got peo-

ple interested in looking at the skies. Before scientists studied the heavens, astrologers did.

Everyone's birthday falls within one of the signs of the zodiac, and some people say your sign determines your personality. They insist that people born under Aries, the Ram sign, are strong and energetic—like a ram. Those born under the sign of Taurus, the Bull, are said to be especially stubborn. Find your birth sign or a friend's on this page and see if you agree.

Deep-Space Dictionary

★★★★★★★★★★★★★★★★★★★★★★★★★

ecliptic The great, imaginary band around the earth marking the course traveled by the sun and planets.
astrology The study of the effects of stars and other objects in space on people's lives.
horoscope A prediction, based on the positions of the stars and planets, of what we can expect in our future.

TAURUS
the Bull

Alongside the Ram is the Bull, or Taurus (*TORE-us*). Part of Taurus is made up of the Pleiades (*PLEE-a-dees*), a beautiful cluster of very young stars. (Only 50 million years old—that's young in terms of the universe.)

Early Greeks believed that Taurus represented a creature that was actually half-man, half-bull. Later the story changed, and Taurus was thought to represent the god Zeus, who once dressed himself in a bull's hide in order to win the heart of princess Europa, who owned a herd of bulls. She fell in love with him, and he dashed into the sky with her on his back. The Taurus constellation doesn't look much like a bull, but if you look closely you can make out his long horns stretching out above Orion's outstretched arm.

ARIES *the Ram*

The first constellation of the zodiac is called Aries (*AIR-ees*), which is Latin for Ram.

According to Greek legend, a man named Aries had a magic coat of sheep's wool that allowed him to fly. He used the coat to rescue a prince and princess, Phrixus (*FRICK-sus*)and Helle (*HELL-uh*), from their evil stepmother. But Helle lost hold of the coat as they flew, and fell into the ocean to her death. Only Phrixus survived. If you look closely at Aries, you can see its two brightest stars right at the tips of the ram's horns.

Star Finding

Aries and Taurus are best spotted around the month of December. Locate them on your Star Finder and look for them in the southern half of the sky. Finding Orion helps—he seems to be aiming his arrow right at Taurus the Bull.

74

with his brother so that they could both live forever. You can see them up in the sky—they look like two stick figures holding on to each other.

CANCER the Crab

The Greeks envisioned Cancer as a crab that grabbed hold of the warrior Hercules (we learned about him earlier) as he battled a giant water snake. Hera (*HAIR-uh*), an enemy of Hercules, rewarded the crab by placing it forever in the stars. Cancer is another constellation that doesn't look much like its name, but look closely and you might be able to make out its claws.

GEMINI *the Twins*

The Twins, also known as Gemini (*JEM-in-eye*), is a constellation that contains the two very bright stars Pollux (*PAHL-ucks*) and Castor (*CAST-or*). Because they appear in the Gemini constellation, these stars were given names in keeping with the ancient Greek legend of Gemini.

The Greeks believed that Castor and Pollux were twin brothers. Pollux was an immortal (a god who will live forever), and Castor a mortal (a regular person who is born and dies). The two brothers were so close that Pollux was given special permission from the god Zeus to share some of his powers

Star Finding

Gemini and Cancer are easiest to find in February. They both lie east of Taurus. If you drew an imaginary line between the Big Dog and the Pole Star, the Gemini Twins would be halfway in between. Because its stars are so faint, Cancer the Crab is probably the hardest constellation to find in the night sky. Binoculars will help. Keep in mind that it is just east of the easy-to-find Twins and right below the Great Bear. A famous hazy cluster of stars, the Beehive, lies near where Cancer's claws branch out.

VIRGO
the Virgin

The Virgin, or Virgo, is the biggest constellation in the zodiac—and it's the only woman. According to Greek mythology, Virgo was a young maiden named Astraea who wandered far and wide seeking out fairness and peace. But there was too much war and injustice on Earth so she took to the heavens, where she can still be seen today, stretched out as if she were lying down across a great, wide portion of the sky.

LEO *the Lion*

The Greeks said that Hercules fought Leo the Lion as a test of strength. The lion's magical pelt (an animal's furry skin) could withstand any weapon, but Hercules beat him anyway, and after that, he wore Leo's pelt as a shield. The lion's spirit drifted into the heavens, where it remains as the constellation Leo. Some people think that the famous Egyptian pyramid we know as the Sphinx was modeled after the crouching Leo constellation. Do you see the resemblance?

Star Finding

Use the Star Finder to look for Leo and Virgo in April, and you'll spot them a bit south of the highest point in the sky over your head. Leo may be the easiest (and most fun) of all the constellations of the zodiac to find. Its stars are bright, and you don't have to use your imagination much to picture the lion. There are thousands of galaxies within the wide outline of Virgo, although of course you'd have to have a very powerful telescope to see them all.

LIBRA *the Scales*

The Scales constellation, or Libra (*LEE-bruh*), looks like an old-fashioned set of scales, the kind that's made of two trays suspended from a long crossbar. Early star gazers believed that the scales of Libra belonged to Virgo, the virgin, and that she used them to measure equality as she wandered the Earth on her search for justice. Libra is another tough constellation to spot—all of its stars are pretty dim. There is one thing particularly special about it, however: among its stars is one with the tongue-twisting name of Zubeneschamali (*zoo-BEN-uh-shuh-MAL-ee*). Not only is that star a mouthful to pronounce, it's the only one that we can spot with our eyes that shines with a greenish light.

Star Finding

Libra and Scorpio are best seen in June, and you'll find them both fairly low in the night sky, down close to the horizon. Look for the star Zubeneschamali at the bottom of the Libra's rightmost scale. Antares in the center of Scorpio's back, near where his claws begin.

Antares is very far away, but it is huge—300 times as wide as our Sun!

Many different cultures around the world have imagined the Scorpio constellation as the same deadly, stinging animal. The Greeks believed it to be a scorpion that attacked and killed the warrior Orion, which explains why Scorpio enters our night sky just as Orion exits—he's fleeing from the horrible creature.

SCORPIO *the Scorpion*

Scorpio the Scorpion is a fun constellation to find, because it really looks like the thing it was named after. If you peer at the stars that make up Scorpio (some call it by its Latin name, Scorpius), it's easy to picture the long, twisting body of a scorpion with a stinger on its tail and pincers near its head. Scorpio also contains the very bright star Antares (*ahn-TAHR-ees*), which is reddish in color, like the planet Mars.

SAGITTARIUS
the Archer

Sagittarius (*SAJ-uh-TARE-ee-us*) the Archer isn't like any archer we know. This one is what's known as a centaur (*SEN-tawr*), a creature with the lower half of a horse and the upper half of a man. The Greeks believed that Sagittarius was once an immortal who would live forever, but then Hercules shot him with a poison arrow. Rather than suffer in pain for all eternity, he gave up his immortality. Now he lives on in the stars, carefully aiming his own bow and arrow.

Star Finding

Use your Star Finder to locate Sagittarius and Capricorn in August, when they're easiest to spot. You'll find them both low in the sky. Sagittarius faces the Scorpion with his arrow drawn and his bow pulled back, ready to fire away. Capricorn is galloping along behind him.

CAPRICORN *the Goat*

Like Cancer the Crab, Capricorn (*KAP-ri-corn*) the Goat is a faint constellation that is not easy to find. It is large, though, and fills a wide section of the summer sky. And Capricorn is more than just a goat. Like Sagittarius the Archer, Capricorn is a combination of two animals in one—he has the tail of a fish and the front legs and head of a goat. Greek legend has it that the god Pan transformed himself into an animal as he dove into the sea in order to escape from a scary monster known as Typhon (*TY-fun*). Pan was halfway into the water when the change took place, so he became half fish, half goat—but at least he survived.

AQUARIUS
the Water Carrier

The Greeks were among many cultures that associated the appearance of Aquarius (*uh-KWARE-ee-us*) with water. In some countries, it is most visible during the rainy season, which might explain what was on the minds of early astronomers who saw a man with an overflowing bucket as they gazed at these stars.

Aquarius is a rather dim constellation that is famous for its meteor showers. The yearly showers known as the Eta Aquarids and the Delta Aquarids appear to originate inside Aquarius. From there, meteors shoot out across the night sky.

Star Finding

Aquarius and Pisces are easiest to spot around September. Pick them out on your Star Finder and look for them in between Pegasus and the southern horizon. And watch for the Eta Aquarids every year on May 5 and the Delta Aquarids on July 29. (For more on meteor showers, see pages 48 and 92.)

PISCES *the Fishes*

The Greeks thought that the two fish in the Pisces (*PIE-sees*) constellation had once been gods that turned themselves into fish to escape from the monster Typhon—the same beast that prompted Capricorn to dive into the water to make his escape. (The creature is said to have had 100 fire-breathing heads, so their fear is understandable!) Pisces looks like a pair of fish at the end of long lines, although the constellation is made up of faint stars and can be pretty hard to make out.

79

Our journey through the sky has shown us all kinds of interesting things—stars, planets, comets and lots of other dazzling objects. Now you can find the brightest stars in the sky, and you've learned to pick out the constellations, too. It's time to put all that knowledge together and look at the great, wide sky all at once.

Many of the stars you see here also appear on the Star Finder, but the view here is closer to how the sky looks from the ground. If you can pick out a constellation in this illustration and then find the same one on the Star Finder, it will help you find the real thing when you go outside to search for stars.

Here are all of the constellations we met, and lots more. (To tell the story of every one would take a much bigger book.)

Once you've figured out which direction is north, see if you can find the stars in the sky that you see in the picture. Or better yet, try and find the Big Dipper and look for the Pole Star nearby. That's the best way of all to find what's called True North.

On the following pages are pictures of the sky at different points throughout the year. Why different views for different times of year? As we've learned, the Earth revolves around the Sun, which means we see different parts of the universe throughout the year when we look to the skies. As the Earth makes its yearly journey around the Sun, the backdrop of stars slowly changes.

North

Cassiopeia

Cygnus

Andromeda

Lyra

Cepheus

Perseus

Hercules

Draco

Ursa Minor

Auriga

Ursa Major

Taurus

Corona Bor.

Gemini

East

Boötes

Cancer

West

Ophiuchus

Leo

Orion

Libra

Canis Major

Virgo

Hydra

Corvus

Puppis

Centaurus

Vela

South

If you want to imagine how the Earth's view of the stars changes as it circles the Sun, here's another way to look at it: Think about standing in a large, round room with a wide painting that stretches all the way around the room, curving so that it makes a complete circle. As you travel around the room, you come across different parts of the picture.

The Earth travels around the Sun in much the same way, and as it does, the view of the stars we see slowly changes. The Swan is easy to find in the summer, and Orion dominates the view in the winter. After one full trip around the Sun, we're back where we started, and we see the same stars we saw one year earlier.

You can watch the stars move as the Earth revolves around the Sun. Try going outside for two nights in a row, and noting where the stars are in relation to the tallest tree in your yard at exactly 8:30 each night. If you look carefully, you'll notice that the position of the stars is just a little different from the first night to the second.

Every night, each star rises into the sky about four minutes earlier than it did the night before (and sets four minutes earlier, too). In one week, they're rising about a half hour earlier than they did the week before (twenty-eight minutes, to be exact). In a month, any given star is entering the sky a full two hours earlier. And guess what happens in a year? Twelve months times two hours equals twenty-four hours—or one full day. That's why you'll see the very same stars you see tonight in the exact spot one year from now.

THE SKY IN SUMMER

North

Auriga

Perseus

Cassiopeia

Ursa Major

Cepheus

Ursa Minor

Andromeda

Draco

Leo

Hercules

Cygnus

Boötes

Pegasus

Lyra

Virgo

Aquila

Aquarius

Ophiuchus

Corvus

Capricornus

Libra

Centaurus

Scorpius

Sagittarius

South

East

West

But there's more to the stars' movement than just the Earth's revolution around the Sun. Remember that the Earth is rotating, too, constantly spinning on its axis so that it makes a full rotation in 24 hours. The stars you see in the illustrations represent what the sky looks like not only on a specific day, but at a precise time. One hour later, the Earth would have rotated slightly, and the sky would look a little different. Most of the stars would have slid a bit to the west, except for stars nearest the Pole Star, which move very little. Just as the Sun rises in the East and sets in the West, the stars rise and set. But of course it's not the Sun that is moving, or the stars—we are.

Why doesn't the Pole Star seem to move? As we learned, the Pole Star is sometimes called the North Star because when viewed from the Earth, the North Star can always be found to the north. The reason it seems to stay in the same place has something to do with why it always points north. If you were to draw a straight line along the Earth's axis starting at the South Pole, running through the very center of the Earth's core, then out the North Pole and up into the sky, that line would lead almost straight to the Pole Star.

The Earth spins along that axis—as we learned earlier, it rotates—which is why the stars appear to move across the sky over the course of a night. As the planet rotates, the stars appear to travel in a circle, ending up more or less where they started after 24 hours. Imagine holding an umbrella over your head and staring up into it as you slowly spin the handle. The edges of the umbrella would rotate in a circle around you. But the center of the umbrella would stay directly above you. The Pole Star is the same way—except, of course, we're the ones moving, not the sky.

THE SKY IN FALL

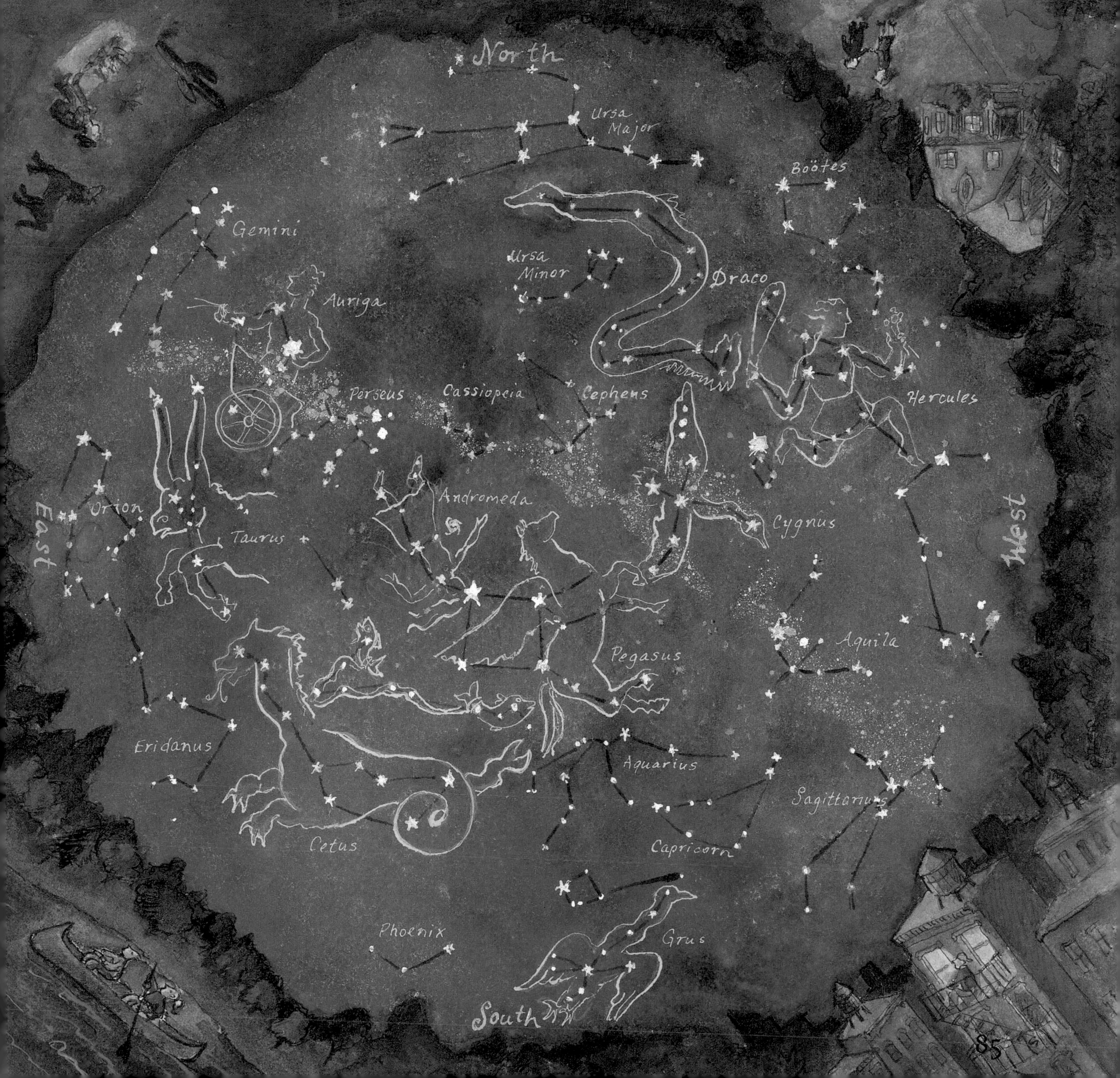

North

Ursa Major

Boötes

Gemini

Ursa Minor

Draco

Auriga

Hercules

Perseus   Cassiopeia   Cepheus

Orion

Andromeda

Cygnus

Taurus

West

East

Pegasus

Aquila

Eridanus

Aquarius

Sagittarius

Cetus

Capricorn

Phoenix

Grus

South

Because the Earth is round, it offers different views of the stars from different places. The sky wraps all the way around the planet, and at every point, there's a different view overhead.

At the North Pole, the Pole Star shines directly overhead, but as you travel south toward the equator, the Pole Star slides farther and farther down toward the horizon. By the time you reach the equator, you can't see the Pole Star at all. At that point, the star would be 90 degrees from the center of the sky overhead, or just about even with the horizon. (Remember learning about measuring degrees earlier?)

A full view of the sky, from the southern horizon to the northern horizon, would cover 180 degrees. But we can only see about 160 of these degrees. We lose about 10 degrees just above the horizon in both directions—20 degrees altogether—because the atmosphere close to the Earth is too dense and scatters the stars' light. Hills and buildings get in the way, too.

But just as the Pole Star can't be seen below the equator, there are stars and constellations that can't be seen if you're closer to the North Pole. The constellation known as the Southern Cross is one of these hard-to-find stars in the North. (In most places above the equator, in fact, it's impossible to see.) But it's very easy to find below the equator, which is why both Australia and New Zealand—countries located "Down Under" the equator—feature the Southern Cross on their flags.

TO THE STARS AND BACK AGAIN

We've just about reached the end of our trip through the universe. You've learned a lot, but remember, we've only begun to start unraveling the many mysteries of the cosmos. Think of all the things that are still out there, waiting to be explained—black holes, gravity and the fabled Planet X, to name just a few.

And don't forget all the things we don't even know that we don't know. New mysteries tend to spring up just when we're figuring out the answer to one of the old ones. Maybe someday you'll be one of the people discovering those answers.

You've got plenty to keep you busy until then—studying the constellations, getting a peek at an eclipse or maybe even a comet, and following the ongoing march into space that nations around the world are pursuing. That's the most amazing thing about the wide universe around us: there's so much still to learn, and new secrets are uncovered every day.

A BRIEF HISTORY OF SPACE

c. 2000 B.C. (around 2000 B.C.) Stonehenge, a collection of giant stone slabs set upright in a wide circle, is built in what is now Wiltshire, England. We're not sure who built it or why, but scientists believe the structure was used to monitor the movement of the Sun and Moon.

c. 400 B.C. Egyptians record the motion of the Sun and Moon on stone tablets that we can still study today. The tablets contain information that earlier astronomers had collected.

c. 350 B.C. Chinese astronomer Shih Shen logs about 800 stars in the first known star catalog.

c. 500 B.C. – A.D. 400 Greek astronomers study the stars and planets, and the Earth's relation to them. Pythagoras and his followers teach that the Earth is round. Ptolemy studies the motion of the planets, and Aristotle collects the work of other astronomers, creating a valuable resource for centuries to come.

c. 1000 Arabic astronomer al-Sufi records information about hundreds of stars in his star catalog, and spots the first galaxy outside our own, the Andromeda galaxy.

1543 Nicolaus Copernicus introduces the revolutionary idea that the Earth and other planets actually orbit around the Sun. Not everyone believes him.

c. 1600 Danish astronomer Tycho Brahe works to figure out whether the Sun revolves around the Earth or the other way around.
His assistant Johannes Kepler helps to discover that the planets do orbit the Sun, in an elliptical shape.

1609 Italian astronomer Galileo Galilei perfects the telescope and is able to use it to prove that the planets do revolve around the Sun. This gets him in trouble with people who think that goes against the teachings of the Bible.

1682 Edmond Halley tracks a comet and determines that it makes an appearance approximately every 76 years—meaning that it must be orbiting around the Sun. (When it reappears on schedule in 1758 it is named Halley's Comet.)

1687 According to legend, Sir Isaac Newton gets hit on the head by a falling apple and comes up with the explanation for gravity—or why we don't fall up.

1774 Astronomer Charles Messier publishes a catalog of nebulae and star clusters. Unofficially, these things are known as Messier Objects, and officially, the first letter of his name is still used to identify them—the Andromeda galaxy is also called M31.

1789 William Herschel, who discovered Uranus in 1782, builds a giant telescope that he uses to study the moons of Saturn, examine binary stars, discover thousands of new nebulae and explore many other space mysteries.

1864 John Frederick Herschel, William's son, publishes his own catalog, introducing many more previously unknown nebulae. (His aunt and William's sister, Caroline, was also a noted astronomer, and discovered eight comets.)

1918 The Hooker Telescope begins operating in California. Edwin Hubble would use this in the 1920s to make many discoveries that are an important part of the Big Bang theory.

 1926 Robert Goddard, an American scientist, launches the first modern rocket using liquid fuel, opening up the possibility of space travel.

1930 Clyde Tombaugh, an Arizona astronomer, discovers the furthest planet in our Solar System, a small, frigid place called Pluto.

1957 The Soviets launch *Sputnik 1*, the first spaceship to orbit the Earth.

1961 Soviet cosmonaut Yuri Gagarin becomes the first man to travel into space. American Alan Shepard follows him less than one month later.

1962 John Glenn becomes the first American to orbit the Earth, which he circles three times in under five hours.

1962 The *Mariner 2* probe leaves on its trip past Venus. A half-dozen other *Mariner* probes will explore Venus, Mars and Mercury over the next ten years.

 1969 American astronaut Neil Armstrong becomes the first human being to step on the surface of the moon.

1971 The Soviets send up the first space station, *Salyut*. The United States follows two years later with its own version, Skylab.

1972 The first of two *Pioneer* probes heads toward Jupiter, becoming the first spacecraft to travel through the asteroid belt between Mars and Jupiter.

1977 Two *Voyager* probes head away from the Sun to explore Jupiter, Saturn, Uranus, Neptune—and beyond.

1981 The United States launches the first Space Shuttle, *Columbia*, a ship that can carry up to ten astronauts into space, stay for more than a week, then return to Earth intact.

1986 The Space Shuttle *Challenger* explodes after takeoff, killing seven astronauts.

 1990 The Hubble Space Telescope is sent into orbit, offering views of the universe that are much clearer than the views from Earth.

1994 Work begins on the International Space Station, and continues to this day.

1997 The United States sends the rover *Sojourner* to Mars aboard the Pathfinder spacecraft. The *Sojourner* travels around the surface of Mars and collects information and pictures for three months (but doesn't run into any Martians).

 1998 At age 77, John Glenn returns to space aboard the Space Shuttle Discovery. The first American to orbit the Earth becomes the oldest person ever in space.

2003 The Space Shuttle *Columbia* disintegrates on its way back to the Earth after sixteen days in space, killing all seven astronauts on board.

2005 The United States launches the Space Shuttle *Discovery*. It is the first shuttle flight since the *Columbia* disaster.

2010 Space Shuttle *Discovery* returns to space for 10 days. It is the first time that four women are in space at the same time.

NIGHT SIGHTS

FINDING THE PLANETS

Below are the best times to look for the planets. Find the widest, flattest space you can find, with the fewest obstacles between you and the horizon. Mercury and Venus are easiest to see in the evening right after sundown (or in the morning just before dawn). To spot those two planets, it's especially important that you have a clear view of the western horizon without many trees or buildings in the way. The best way to spot Mars, Jupiter or Saturn is to look for them in the constellations listed below.

Mercury

Remember that Mercury's orbit is closest to the Sun, which makes it hard to see—the Sun's light outshines it. So the best time to look for Mercury is right after the Sun goes down or right before it rises, when it is just beneath the horizon. Look for Mercury just above the horizon to the west.

2010: late March and early April

2011: mid- to late March

2012: early March; mid- to late June

2013: mid- February; early to mid- June

2014: late January into February; mid- to late May

Venus

Venus is bright—brighter than any object in the sky besides the Moon—so you shouldn't have trouble spotting

it. Like Mercury, Venus's orbit means it never strays too far from the Sun. Look for it above the western horizon right after sundown during the following months:

2010: March-September

2011: November-December

2012: January-May

2013: May-December

Mars

Mars, too, is sometimes too close to the Sun to spot. But at other times it can be seen wandering through the constellations, following its path along the ecliptic as it makes its way around the Sun.

2010: Cancer (January-April); Leo (June-July); Virgo (August)

2011: Taurus (June-July); Gemini (August-September); Leo (November-December)

2012: Leo (January-June); Virgo (July-August); Scorpio (October)

2013: Taurus (July); Gemini (August); Leo (October-November)

2014: Virgo (January-July); Scorpio (September-October); Capricorn (December)

Jupiter

Leave it to the Sun to outshine Jupiter, too, from time to time. The best place to spot the biggest planet is when it passes through the following constellations, after the Sun has gone below the western horizon.

2010: Capricorn (January)
2011: Aquarius/Pisces (March)
2012: Aries (June-December)
2013: Gemini (July-December)
2014: Cancer (February-June)

Saturn

You won't be able to make out its rings without a telescope, but you can find Saturn as it passes through the constellations of the ecliptic.

2010: Virgo
2011: Virgo
2012: Virgo
2013: Libra (January-June)
2014: Libra

 ## CATCHING A COMET

If you wait until 2061, you'll be able to see Halley's Comet as it makes another pass through the skies above the Earth. Or if you're really patient, you can catch the Hale-Bopp Comet when it makes its next visit in the year 4397. But other comets will come by before then. We don't always know when the next one will show up, but astronomers usually spot one—and spread the word—in plenty of time for us to see it before it zooms out of our sky. Check astronomy magazines and Web sites for updates on comets that we can spot from here on Earth.

CLASHES OF TITANS

Every now and then, two or more planets appear to pass one another in a meeting called a conjunction. This is an especially fun time to try and spot them—two planets (or more) for the price of one! Look for the following conjunctions just after sundown:

April 19, 2011: Mercury, Jupiter, Mars
May 11, 2011: Venus, Jupiter, Mars
May 27, 2013: Mercury, Jupiter, Venus
March 4, 2015: Venus, Uranus, Mars
August 28, 2016: Mercury, Jupiter, Venus

A SHOT AT A SHOOTING STAR

As we learned before, the best time to see meteors or "shooting stars" is during a meteor shower. Here are some of the best ones, and the approximate dates of their peaks:

January 3: Quadrantids
August 12: Perseids
December 14: Geminids
May 5: Eta Aquarids
July 29: Delta Aquarids
October 21: Orionids
December 22: Ursids

LEARN MORE ABOUT IT

ASTRONOMY AND SPACE SCIENCE

Campbell, Ann-Jeanette. *The New York Public Library Amazing Space*. New York: John Wiley, 1997.

Encyclopedia Americana. Danbury, Connecticut: Grolier, 2002.

Lippincott, Kristin. *Astronomy*. London: Dorling Kindersley, 2000.

New Encyclopedia Britannica. Chicago: Encyclopedia Britannica, Inc., 1998.

Odenwald, Sten. *Back to the Astronomy Café*. Cambridge: Westview Press, 2003.

World Book Encyclopedia. Chicago: World Book Inc., 2000, 2002.

STARGAZING

Dickinson, Terence. *Nightwatch: A Practical Guide for Viewing the Universe*. Ontario: Firefly Books, 2006.

Discovery Channel Night Sky. New York: Discovery Books, 1999.

Graun, Ken. *Touring the Universe: A Practical Guide to Exploring the Cosmos thru 2017*. Tucson: Ken Press, 2002.

Rey, H.A. *Find the Constellations*. Boston: Houghton Mifflin, 1982.

Rey, H.A. *The Stars: A New Way to See Them*. Boston: Houghton Mifflin, 1980.

Thompson, C.E. *Glow-In-the-Dark Constellations: A Field Guide for Young Stargazers*. New York: Grosset & Dunlap, 1989.

STAR STORIES

Leach, Maria, ed. *Dictionary of Folklore, Mythology and Legend*. New York: Funk & Wagnalls, 1950.

Dixon-Kennedy, Mike. *Encyclopedia of Greco-Roman Mythology*. Santa Barbara, California: ABC-CLIO, 1998.

INTERNET RESOURCES

www.astronomy.com

www.astronomynow.com

www.dustbunny.com/afk

www.infoplease.com

www.kidsastronomy.com

www.nasa.gov

space.about.com

www.space.com

starchild.gsfc.nasa.gov

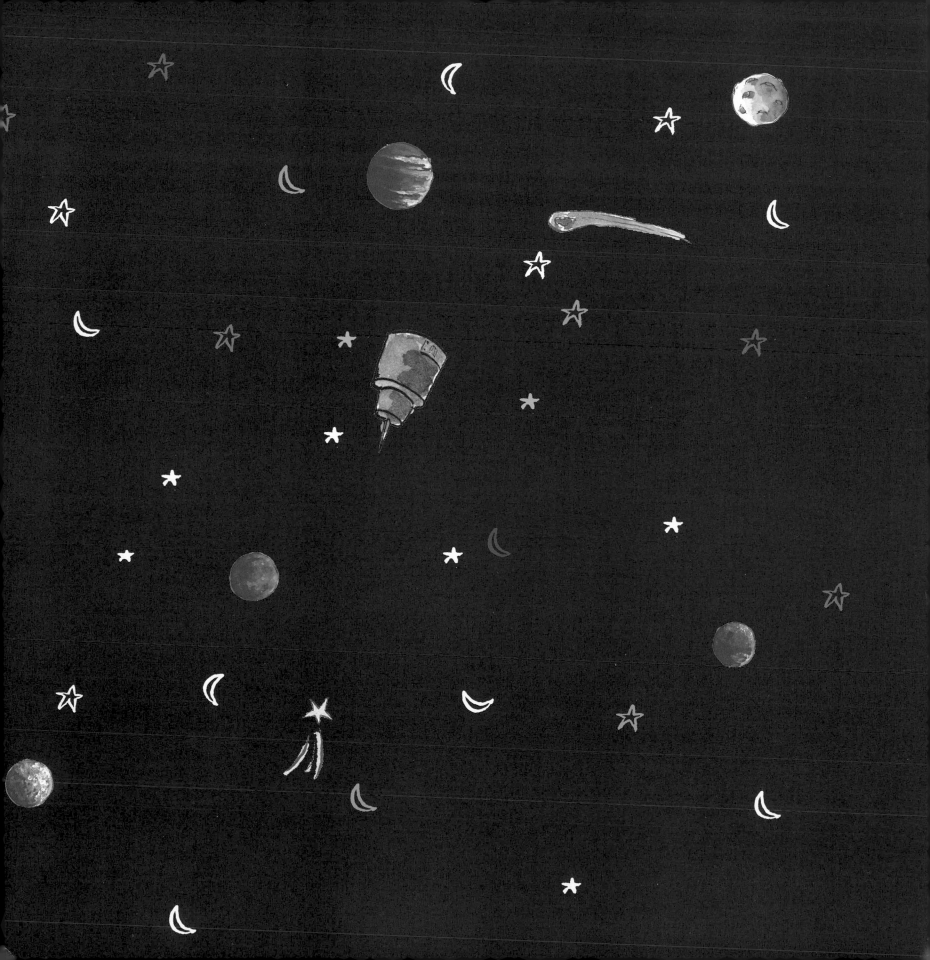